The *Unauthorized* Legoland Guidebook

How to Save Money and Have More Fun at Legoland, California

By: Bridget Smith

A Family Adventure Guidebook

Family Adventure Guidebooks
An imprint of Class7Training LLC

The Unauthorized Legoland Guidebook - How to Save Money and Have More Fun at Legoland, California by Bridget Smith

First edition – September 2008
Copyright © 2008 by Class7Training LLC.
Cover photo credit: Brian Stringfellow
Printed in the United States of America
ISBN 978-0-615-25501-9

Acknowledgements

Many thanks to my best friends, Irene and Inga, for the cheerful support that you provided for this project.

Thanks to Brian Stringfellow, my excellent cover photographer who managed to take a great picture before the sun set.

Thanks to my husband, Ken, editor, formatter, business partner, and friend.

Thank to my dad and mom, John and Lee Gillin for helping to keep the house running and the grandkids entertained while I immersed myself in this project.

Thanks to my editors and fellow moms Lisa Witz and Deana Reynolds. Hope I can return the favor some day.

Dear: Justin, Destiny, and Jared,

Thanks for all your help writing this book. I had so much fun seeing Legoland with you. You are the inspiration for this book, and pretty much everything else in my life. I look forward to our next adventure!

Love,
Mom

Contents

I. Introduction

My son Justin is a diehard Lego fan. Most of my husband's family lives in the San Diego Area. Still, we didn't visit Legoland California until Justin was 6 years-old. That first day I visited the park, I had to wonder, "What took us so long?" This was the perfect theme park for preschoolers and school-age children. There was an amazing assortment of fun, hands on activities for every age group. Even waiting in line was less painful, since many of the more popular rides included Lego play areas for kids. Almost every ride or attraction was interactive and encouraged creativity. Around every corner there were opportunities, to climb, splash, build, or create.

A year later our family moved to Carlsbad, California, a few blocks away from Legoland. We became Legoland members and spent the summer exploring this extraordinary theme park. Our family includes a 3 year-old, a 4 year-old, and a 9 year-old. With such a wide age range we had a chance to discover rides and attractions that we could enjoy together as a family. We also identified those that were more appropriate for a Mom and big kid date. Time and again I have marveled at how much Legoland has to offer every member of our family. Just when I think I have explored every corner of the theme park, I discover something new.

Be aware, that Legoland is a very different theme park concept. It is not all about the rides! For older kids and adults the choices for thrill rides is very limited. You should head to Legoland expecting to play with lots of Lego bricks, see some shows, get very wet, and work together to put out imaginary fires. I appreciate that this is not a passive theme park. You don't just sit back and be entertained. When you enjoy rides like the Fun Town Fire Academy or activities like the Build and Test, you and your family are actively engaged in working together and having fun.

This guide is designed to help your family make the most of your visit to Legoland California. Although ticket prices seem steep, I'll let you know where you can look for discounted admission, how to save money once you're in the park, and even how to visit for free! I have suggestions for what to ride, what to see, where to shop and eat, and when to go. The entire Smith family has contributed to this guide, so you can receive a kid's perspective on fun rides and attractions for every age group. I've also included some suggestions for rides and attractions that are fun for the whole family so no one has to be left out.

Whether you go for one day or become a Legoland member this guide will help you to save money and have more fun as you explore the park. So pack your suitcase or pack up the minivan and head off on your Legoland Adventure!

II.   Getting Tickets and Passes

A.   *Ticket Window Prices*

Ticket	Child (3-12 yrs old)	Adult (13-59 yrs old)	Senior (60-and-over)
1-day Legoland	$49.95	$59.95	$49.95
1-day Sea Life	$11.95	$18.95	$15.95
1-day Hopper	$59.95	$69.95	$59.95
2-day Legoland	$62.95	$74.95	$62.95
2-day Hopper	$64.95	$79.95	$64.95
1-day Legoland Premium Play Pass	$100	$120	$100

Premium Play Pass

Hate waiting in line? Here's you chance to go to the front of the line every time. Legoland is offering a new kind of Premium Play Pass ticket which sells for $120 for adults and $100 kids. This ticket gives you guaranteed front of the line privileges. If you want to use your ticket to ride the same ride again you have to wait an hour between rides.

Only 60 of these tickets are issued per day, so it does make you a member of an exclusive club and ensures that your wait is very short (as long as all sixty people don't decide to ride the Safari Jeeps at the same time!) On most days this ticket is an indulgence rather than a necessity. However, if you are willing and able to pay the high price of this ticket, it might come in handy during holidays like the Fourth of July, at special events that attract a lot of attendees (Star Wars Day) and on crowded summer days. If you want to take advantage of the Premium Play Pass benefits, make sure you arrive early in the day. On the Fourth of July this year, these passes sold out.

1 and 2-Day Tickets

You can purchase 1- and 2- day tickets online at www.legoland.com or as soon as you arrive at the park. Lines can be long, so it might be worth buying ahead of time. Park Hopper tickets are also available if you want to visit Legoland and the Sea Life Aquarium on the same day. These might be a good idea if you plan to go to the aquarium. The Sea Life Aquarium is not a full day activity.

Ticket holders can upgrade their tickets to a second day before leaving the park. With any paid admission ticket the upgrade would be $15. The cost of an upgrade for a complimentary ticket would be $37 (adults) and $31 (child). The second day must be used within 7 days of the initial visit. It is also possible to upgrade your ticket to a Park Hopper Pass that allows you to visit the Sea Life Aquarium in addition to Legoland.

B.   *Discounted Tickets*

Legoland tickets can be pricy, but there are a few ways to get discounts.

Online Auctions

Legoland Membership Plus and Ambassador Memberships include one day guest passes which can sometimes be found for sale on San Diego Craigslist at www.craigslist.org or on eBay at www.ebay.com. These are also great places to find promotional coupons, such as pay an adult admission, bring a child for free. These coupons are given away at local attractions like The Flower Fields at Carlsbad Ranch (see page 108) and local fast food restaurants (see page 115). If these are not available in your area, it may be worth purchasing one from an online source.

Costco 1-Day Tickets

If you are a Costco member and only plan to visit for one day, you should purchase the ticket from Costco if you can. Costco Wholesale located minutes away from Legoland on Palomar Airport Road sells 1-day tickets that include a round of golf at the Wild Woods Golf miniature golf course in Legoland for $44.99 (adult) and $35.99

(child/senior admission). This is about $15 off of the usual price and also includes the free round of golf. Tickets are available at these prices online as well at www.costco.com.

Go San Diego Card

Planning a vacation to San Diego? If you are going to visit museums and attractions in addition to Legoland you might want to purchase a Go San Diego Card. This card gives you admission to a wide variety of museums and attractions including Sea World, The San Diego Zoo, The San Diego Wild Animal Park and Knott's Soak City Water Park. Adult admission prices range from $89.99 for a two day card to $189.99 for a seven day card. The card also gives discounts for many local restaurants and stores.

Brickmaster Club

Plan ahead before you leave for your Legoland vacation. Join the Brickmaster Club for $39.99 plus tax, shipping, and handling and receive one free admission to Legoland. Plus you also get 6 Lego sets mailed to your home and a free subscription to Brickmaster magazine. See http://shop.lego.com/brickmaster/ for details.

Other Discounts

As I mentioned before, local fast food restaurants, The San Diego Zoo and Wild Animal Park, and The Flower Fields at Carlsbad Ranch sometimes give out Legoland Coupons. If you are in the area and haven't purchased tickets ahead of time you may want to keep your eyes open.

- ☐ Some San Diego **Vons Grocery Stores** offer discounted passes throughout the year as well as periodic special promotions (This spring tickets were 50% off). If you need to do some grocery shopping before you go to Legoland you might want to be on the lookout for tickets.
- ☐ Sign your Lego fan up for a free **Lego Magazine** subscription and keep an eye out for Legoland discount coupons: http://club1.lego.com/en-US/legomagazine/default.aspx.
- ☐ **AAA members** may be eligible for $10 off of admission if they show their AAA card.
- ☐ **Airline employees** get a discount of 20% off of admission for up to six tickets per visit. They must show a valid employee airline ID.
- ☐ **Active Military personnel** get 10% off of a one day admission ticket with a valid military I.D. Additional discounts may be available on base.
- ☐ Sometimes l**arge employers** offer discounted passes to various theme parks. Check with your employee benefits office.
- ☐ Season pass holders at local water parks such as **The Wave** in Vista and **Wild Rivers Water Park** in Irvine may receive free admission to Legoland during certain times of the year. See the websites of these parks for more information.

 See our website:
www.FamilyAdventureGuidebooks.com for links to more discounts.

C.   *Visiting Legoland for Free!*

Free? Yes, you heard right...FREE! The catch is you will only have a little more than an hour to visit the park. Legoland stops checking tickets and charging for parking an hour before it closes. The intention is for people to go in and shop at the Big Shop. If you live in the area, want to preview the park before purchasing tickets or passes, or have always wanted to see Miniland, you can slip in for a free visit. The rides will shut down exactly at closing time, but the park will be open for another half an hour after closing. This is not the way to see the whole park, but if you plan ahead and rush you can catch a ride or two before you have to head home.

D.   *Membership*

If you enjoy Legoland so much that you want to purchase an annual pass there are several ways that you can save. If you have already visited Legoland and want to purchase passes directly from Legoland use your ticket stub to upgrade before you leave the park. Legoland will deduct the cost of the original ticket from the price of membership. Complimentary 1-day tickets have an upgrade value of $10 towards the purchase of a membership.

There are many levels of membership available especially now that Legoland is forming resort partnerships and with the recent opening of the new Sea Life Aquarium. In most cases, I would recommend a combination of Standard Member and Membership Plus passes. Membership Plus passes provide free parking (usually $10 a visit) provided the member is riding in your car. If you are going to visit Legoland a lot, it makes sense to buy one Membership Plus pass for the family member who will be attending Legoland most frequently. My friend, Naomi, purchased the Membership Plus pass for her Legoland fan. When she drives to Legoland she gets free parking. When her son attends Legoland with visiting family and friends, they can also show his pass for free parking. Naomi has a 13 year-old daughter who is less interested in Legoland. Her son's Membership Plus pass included a free ticket, so the 13 year-old could join everyone for a family day at Legoland.

Comparison of Legoland Memberships

Membership	Term	Sea Life Admission	Free Parking	Complimentary 1-day Tickets	Legoland Discount Dinning / Shopping	Child or Senor	Adult
3-Month Costo	3 mo	No	No	No	No	$42.99	$51.99
Model Mom	1 yr Thurs only	No	Yes Thurs only	No	20% / 0% Thurs only	-	$59.95
Military	1 yr	No	Yes	1	20% / 10%	-	$95
Standard	1 yr	No	No	No	None	$89	$115
Plus	1 yr	No	Yes	1	20% / 10%	$114	$138
Resort	1 yr	Yes	Yes	1	20% / 10%	$139	$159
Ambassador	Life	No	Yes*	4	20% / 10%	$2,000	$2,000
Ambassador Resort	Life	Yes	Yes*	4	20% / 10%	$2,550	$2,550

* Preferred Parking

Costco 3-Month Membership

Costco has affordable three month passes so you can enjoy Legoland all summer long for less than a full priced one day ticket. Current prices are $51.99 for adults (13-59) and $42.99 for children/seniors. Be sure to purchase one premium pass at Legoland for your family if you want to get free parking. If you are not a

Costco member you can still purchase discounted Legoland tickets ahead of time at www.costco.com. Just be prepared to pay a 5% surcharge as a non-member.

Model Mom Membership

If you have a child under the age of four and live close to Legoland or are visiting San Diego for an extended period you might want to consider purchasing a Model Mom pass. Model Mom membership is $59.95 per year. Kids under the age of 3 are admitted to the park for free. If your child is over 3 years-old you would need to purchase a Standard or Membership Plus membership. The Model Mom pass gives you free admission, parking on any Thursday, and a 20% discount at all restaurants along with a free subscription to Lego Magazine. It is not valid for any other day of the week. Every Thursday Legoland offers fun activities such as stroller exercise, music or crafts for the 4-and-under age group which Model Mom members and other visitors with small children are invited to attend. Most Model Mom activities take place in the room next to Build & Test. Stroller Strides meets at The Beginning. See the Legoland website for the Model Mom schedule.

Military Membership

Military memberships are offered at $95 which is a significant discount and include free parking and a free 1-day ticket.

Standard Membership

Current prices for Standard Membership passes are $115 for adults and $89 for children and seniors.

Standard membership is the most affordable option but it does not include free parking or dining and retail discounts. The other drawback is that this membership level is not eligible for monthly payments. This is a good option for the adults in your family since in most cases only one Membership Plus is needed per family.

Membership Plus

Current pricing for Membership Plus is $138 for adults and $113 for children and seniors.

Membership Plus offers all the Standard membership benefits, but also gives the holder free parking, a 20% discount on food and a 10% discount on retail purchases. Purchasing passes for the whole family at once can be hard on the budget. Membership Plus offers a monthly payment plan option. Just realize that you are entering into a year contract and that after that year, it is up to you to cancel the membership. It will not expire and your credit card will continue to be charged until you contact Legoland to cancel. This is a reasonably easy process and can be done by phone or e-mail. You might want to check ahead of time to find out your monthly renewal date.

 Note that for both the Standard and Membership Plus memberships seniors are charged a child's rate so be sure to let Legoland know if you are old enough to be a senior! (In the Legoland universe, this means age 60+.)

Resort Membership

Current Pricing for Resort Membership is $159 for adults and $139 for children and seniors.

With the construction of the new Sea Life Aquarium and the formation of a partnership with neighboring resorts, Legoland has introduced the new Resort membership. If you are a big Legoland fan and are planning to make multiple trips to Legoland that will include hotel stays at the Grand Pacific Palisades Resort and the Sheraton Carlsbad Resort and Spa, you might want to consider this membership. It also is the membership choice for those who want to visit the Sea Life Aquarium on a regular basis. Resort membership includes unlimited admission to both Legoland and the Sea Life Aquarium, free parking, a one day guest pass, a 20% discount on food and a 10% discount on retail purchases at both Legoland and the Sea Life Aquarium, discounted admission to both venues for your invited guests, as well as special discounts at the Sheraton Carlsbad Resort and a waiver of the $9 per day resort fee and free breakfast for two at the Grand Pacific Palisades Resort.

Ambassador Membership

Ready to enjoy a lifetime of fun at Legoland? For $2,000 you can become a Legoland Ambassador Pass member. This gives you unlimited entrance to all Legoland Theme Parks around the world. You will also receive free Ambassador parking and four additional Legoland admissions yearly for life. Legoland Ambassador Members enjoy an exclusive building session with a Lego Master Builder. You also receive the same perks as Membership Plus members.

Legoland California Ambassador Resort Membership

Until May of 2009 you can upgrade your Ambassador Membership to an Ambassador Resort Membership for $2,300. After May 2009, the price will be $2,550.

These members receive the same perks as Ambassador Members, but also receive free admission to the Sea Life Aquarium and two free Sea Life Aquarium guest passes per year.

Member Perks

Most members receive information about special promotions and discounts throughout the year. Last year these included, guest admission coupons that allowed us to bring friends and family who were not pass members to Legoland. We received two sets of coupons, one in the winter just in time to enjoy Legoland's Christmas and New Year's Celebrations and one in the spring. Thanks to the coupons we headed to Legoland with the grandparents on Christmas after the last present was unwrapped.

If you find yourself with an extra Legoland ticket from your Membership Plus, Ambassador, or Resort membership, you might want to consider selling it on San Diego Craigslist. Tickets go for $20-40 each depending on the supply available at the time you are posting.

III.   Planning Your Visit

A.   *When to Go: Times of Year*

Legoland's attendance varies widely due to the day of the week and the season. If you plan accordingly, you may feel like you have your own private theme park!

Carlsbad, CA Weather Averages[1]

		Jan	Feb	Mar	Apr	May	Jun	Jul	Aug	Sept	Oct	Nov	Dec
Temp °F	Average	55	55	57	59	62	66	69	71	71	66	60	55
	High	66	68	68	71	72	76	81	83	82	78	72	67
	Low	43	44	46	48	53	56	60	61	59	54	48	43
Rain Fall in.		3.0	2.3	2.7	1.0	-	-	-	-	-	-	1.6	1.8

- Less than 0.5 in.

Summer (June – August)

For most of June Legoland stays open until 6 pm. During July and August Legoland is open until 8 pm. Most of the water attractions are available during this season. Evening is an excellent time to visit Legoland after the crowds have gone home so plan to stay late.

Summer is Legoland's peak season, and the park can be really busy especially on weekends. The good news is that almost all of the rides and attractions will be available during your visit and the park is open 7 days a week. Saturday almost any time of year is usually the busiest day. If you plan to visit on a Saturday, arrive early, use good parking strategies (see page 43), plan to spend more time at the attractions that don't require waiting in line, and head to areas like Fun Town, Castle Hill, or Land of Adventure upon arrival, then move back towards the entrance. Mid week (Tuesday-Thursday) can be less crowded. If you are planning a trip in June, make sure you bring a sweater. Carlsbad "June

---

[1] Data from WeatherReports.com

Gloom" is notorious. Some days the fog does not burn off at all. In general, the fog starts burning off by 9 am late summer and into the fall, so July and August are better bets if you want to enjoy Legoland on a sunny day.

Off Season (September to May)

In general, the park is closed on Tuesdays and Wednesdays during the off season and is open from 10 am-5 pm on other days. Expect some attractions to be closed. From the beginning of September to the beginning of November Pirate Shores will be open from 10 am-5 pm. The park may be open on Tuesday or Wednesday as well as longer hours during holiday breaks and other special events so be sure to check the calendar on the website. You may be pleasantly surprised to find that you will be able to stay late at Legoland.

Off Season weekends outside of school vacations, are good times to hit Legoland. However, expect some attractions to be closed, especially the water attractions. Legoland is a great park because there are fun indoor and outdoor activities. Carlsbad has mild weather, and even during the rainy season, the rain is intermittent. Legoland staff has informed me during the off season Sundays are some of the least crowded days at the park. Weekdays off season are also great times to visit.

Holidays

Legoland is always a wonderful place to visit, but during holidays and special events it really shines.

This past year I spent Mother's Day, Independence Day, and Christmas Day at Legoland. I was pleasantly surprised by the lack of crowds on Christmas and Mother's Day. When everyone is busy celebrating with brunches and present opening, get away to Legoland!

On the Fourth of July the skies light up with fireworks and the sound of patriotic music fills the air. You can even celebrate our nation's birthday by watching the fireworks sitting by "Washington DC" in Miniland, always a great spot for a social studies lesson. The Fourth of July does get very busy. Legoland "model citizens" reported that by afternoon the rides were crowded and things were sold out throughout the park.

The fall and winter holidays bring fun and excitement to the Lego Universe. During the weekends leading up to Halloween, kids can enjoy trick or treating for stickers, Lego bricks and other treats at gaily decorated booths from costumed cast members. Other fun activities include costume contests and scavenger hunts. Sections of Legoland are open late for twilight enjoyment. On Saturdays in October some parts of the park are open from 5pm-9pm for special Halloween activities.

Christmas is a great time for taking photos at Legoland. The whole park is decorated with elaborate Lego holiday decorations. My favorite holiday spot is Miniland where most of the US cities represented are filled with miniature holiday decorations, and festive carolers. Particularly fun sights are the beautifully decorated streets of New Orleans and Rockefeller Center in New York. Green and red fireworks light the night sky on some weekends.

Looking for a kid friendly New Year's celebration? Legoland has you covered with a kids concert at 6 p.m. Lego ball drop is a tribute to Time Square. Christmas/New Years: Dec 26-Dec 31st Legoland is open from 10 am-7 pm.

As you can see Legoland's days of operation and park hours can vary greatly. Make sure you call (760) 918-LEGO or check the website www.Legoland.com\hours to see when the park will be open during your visit.

B.   *Special Events*

Junior Master Model Builder Competition

This event occurs on the first full weekend of every month. In order to participate, stop by the Imagination Zone, and build a Lego model based on the month's theme using the bricks and base plate provided. You can enter your creation on one of three age categories: 9-and-under, 10-15, and 16+ (Even adults can enter in this category.) We attended this event on a summer Saturday. We got to the park at opening and found that it wasn't too crowded. Later in the day it really filled up, so make sure that during high season you come early.

The competition starts at 10 am on both Saturday and Sunday and ends two hours before closing. A Lego Master Builder judges the models on Monday and chooses one for each of the age categories. These winners receive four Legoland tickets and an invitation to attend the Ultimate Build Off event in December of each year. The winning models will also be displayed on www.lego.com.

All the models constructed that month are displayed in cabinets in the Imagination Zone. My son had fun showing off his creation to his friends when they came to visit.

Lego Club Weekend

Lego Club ID card holders as well as current pass holders can receive a free Lego Club Button and a Commemorative Brick. There is a special building event with great prizes and your model may be displayed at legoclub.com. Master Builder University held at the Lego Club House will offer building tips from a real Lego Master Model Builder. Show your button at the Lego Club House and receive a free bag of popcorn when you buy one bag. Buy one pound of pick a brick and you get another ½ pound free! Pick a brick are large bulk bins filled with many unusual Lego bricks and other pieces like flowers and trees.

Our family visited on Lego Club Weekend and attended the building event. It was a fun, but very crowded. (We dropped by around 4 pm.) Be prepared to wait for a spot at the building tables. Try and hit this activity at an off time. If you have kids under 5 you may want to pass. My little ones were overwhelmed by the noise and activity. They also had a scavenger hunt that seemed more appropriate for all ages.

The Lego Club Weekend promotion is valid for kids 16-and-under.

Lego Model Master Builder Session

If you are a Lego Ambassador or Resort Ambassador Member you can participate in an exclusive annual Lego Master Builder session.

Star Wars Day

Holidays aren't the only times of year to have some extra fun at Legoland. Every fall Legoland hosts a Star Wars day. Storm troopers and costumed Star Wars fans descend upon Legoland. There are Star Wars costume contests and builder contests. Elaborate models constructed by adult fans are on display. Most of the Storm Troopers and droids are happy to pose for photos. Lego Star Wars activities are concentrated at the entrance of the park, so once you have seen the models and posed with a Storm Trooper get as far away from the entrance as you can and start playing. Realize that the "big kid" rides and attractions may be busier than usual due to the fact that this event is popular for kids over the age of seven.

The Model Mom Club

The Model Moms Club provides fun activities for kids 4-and-under and their families. Activities include stroller exercise walks, tumbling, crafts, preschool music, and story time. You don't have to be a mom to participate: grandmas, grandpas, dads, and babysitters are welcome too! Be aware that the kiddy rides will be more crowded than usual on Model Mom day.

Keebler Kids Marathon Mile

Have an active kid? Several times a year in the off season Legoland sponsors charity runs and walks. The Carlsbad Marathon includes the Keebler Kids Marathon Mile which will take place at Legoland on January. The event costs $15 dollars per child or adult who is running the course or $20 for a child and non-running adult chaperone. The goodie bag usually includes a free child admission coupon to Legoland good on specific days.

Kids are Worth a Million Day

Want to have fun and contribute to a good cause? The Carlsbad Educational Foundation also holds their annual telethon at the park. Discount tickets are available through local schools and the Foundation itself. If you are visiting the park in the spring it would be wise to check out the Kids are Worth a Million Website www.kidsareworthamillion.com. If you are not purchasing discount tickets to the event, I would recommend avoiding the park on this day. Legoland is abnormally crowded for a spring Saturday and some of the usual shows and amenities will not be available. On the other hand it is a great way to support local schools, get some freebies, and watch talented youngsters including the award winning Carlsbad High Lancer Dancers perform. If you visit on this day, plan to stick to the attractions that don't have lines. We attended the last Kids are Worth a Million Day and spent a fun morning, at the Fun Town playground, splashing in the water at Swabbies Deck and climbing all over The Hideaways.

Birthday Parties

Is your child dreaming of a Legoland Birthday? For the Ultimate Birthday Party you need to invite 10 guests, at full price admission or pay $20 per pass member. The party includes children's meals, a Legoland cake, a private party pavilion, and a Lego toy for every paying child guest.

Another option is a Birthday Express party. You can get discounted Legoland admission and a Legoland birthday cake. At least 10 guests are required.

C.   *When to Go: Times of Day*

Mornings are good times to visit Legoland almost any time of year. Come early and hit the popular rides before the crowds come. Then, hit some of the less visited interactive activities like the Build and Test and Duplo Play Area that don't have lines. Upon arrival, your best strategy may be to head to the back of the park, then work your way to the entrance. Most newly arrived visitors tend to congregate at Dino Island when they first arrive at the park. Be aware that you can walk through

Miniland to get to Knight's Kingdom, and then head left to Pirate's Shore and Fun Town or right to Land of Adventure. Some rides don't open until 10:30 am, but there are many choices available at 10 am in all areas of the park.

Summer evenings are a magical time at Legoland. If you are a pass holder, arrive at 4pm and stay until 8 pm. By that time most visitors have left and you will have the park all to yourself. Miniland is beautiful at twilight, although I hope that someday they will light up Las Vegas!

D.   *Rainy Day Planning*

If you find yourself in Carlsbad on a rainy or overcast day take heart! Bring an umbrella or raincoat and a willingness to be flexible, and be ready for some fun. It seldom rains all day in Carlsbad, California even during the rainy season of January/February/March. You may want to postpone your visit, but if you cannot, I would go ahead and enjoy Legoland.

The usual pattern for rain in Carlsbad is an intense shower, followed by clearing. Find some indoor activities, but keep an eye out the window and after the sun has come out, head for the rides.

 Refer to page 89 for a list of rainy day activities.

E.   *Dog Kennels*

Outdoor shaded kennels are available for FREE on a first-come, first-served basis. A $15 dollar refundable deposit is required. Stop by Guest Services when you enter the park to sign up, pay your deposit, and pick up a key.

IV. Staying in Carlsbad

A. *Legoland Resorts*

Sheraton Carlsbad Resort and Spa
5480 Grand Pacific Drive
Carlsbad, CA
(760) 827-2400

This is one of two official resorts of Legoland. It has Spanish Mediterranean architecture and gorgeous landscaping. Amenities include a pool, hot tub, fitness center, on-site spa, local shuttle, concierge, and tennis courts. Legoland resort pass holders get special perks at this resort including complimentary parking for Legoland visits and spa and dining discounts. I have also heard that Legoland discount coupons are available through the concierge. The resort has a private entrance into Legoland. The hotel's Twenty/20 Grill and Wine Bar has a kids menu with traditional kid favorites like hot dogs, chicken fingers, and pizza.

Grand Pacific Palisades
5805 Armada Dr
Carlsbad, CA
(760) 827-3200

The other official Legoland Resort, Grand Pacific Palisades is just a short walk to Legoland. Legoland Resort pass holders also receive a waiver of the $9 per day resort fee and free breakfast for two when they stay at the Grand Pacific Palisades. Amenities include: an Olympic sized pool for adults only, a family pool and water play park, 3 Jacuzzis, a fitness center, and an activity center with video games and a pool table. The Grand Pacific Palisades also offers a guest shuttle that travels within a five mile radius of the resort (that would include Legoland), as well as lots of fun seasonal activities.

Our family had the opportunity to visit this hotel. All three kids really enjoyed their time at the daycare. The littlest ones watched Dora, played in the toy kitchen, and had pizza for snack. My 9 year-old headed to the older kids club and had fun playing Wii. He also enjoyed the pizza.

It would be a lovely place for the kids to be while the grownups take a swim in the adult pool or enjoy a quiet lunch.

The play park and kids water play area are simple, but everyone looked like they were having fun. The "adult pool" is accessible to families on the weekend, so you have another option when the family pool gets crowded.

B.   *Other Bed and Brick Preferred Hotels*

Bed and Brick hotels offer special packages that include tickets to Legoland. See the Legoland travel website at www.legolandtravel.com for more information.

Carlsbad Inn Beach Resort
3075 Carlsbad Blvd
Carlsbad, CA
(800) 235-3939

This inn, located near downtown Carlsbad, is close to Legoland, the beaches, and Carlsbad Village. Carlsbad Village has many delicious restaurants and quaint shops to explore.

Days Inn Encinitas
133 Encinitas Blvd
Encinitas, CA
(760) 944-0260

This Inn is located three blocks from Moonlight beach one of the nicest family beaches in Encinitas and within 10 miles of Legoland. Amenities include free continental breakfast, in room refrigerator and microwave, free high speed internet, pool, and a complimentary USA Today newspaper. There is a Denny's on site.

Holiday Inn, Carlsbad by the Sea
850 Palomar Airport Rd
Carlsbad, CA
(877) 863-4780

Minutes to Legoland, across the street from The Flower Fields, and a stones throw from the Carlsbad Premium Outlets this hotel has a prime location. It is a former Pea Soup Andersons, so it has a quaint windmill and Danish architecture. TGI Fridays is on-site where kids 12-and-under eat free with a paying adult. Amenities include a health and fitness center and outdoor pool. Free Wi-Fi is also available.

Homewood Suites Carlsbad   2223 Palomar Airport Rd
Carlsbad, CA
(760) 431-2266

This brand new suite hotel is close to McClellan-Palomar Airport and is within easy driving distance of Legoland, The Flower Fields, and the Carlsbad Premium Outlets. Amenities include complimentary hot breakfast, pool with spa, and free internet access throughout the property.

Howard Johnson Encinitas/Legoland   607 Leucadia Blvd.
Encinitas, CA
(760) 944-3800

Located in the quaint beach town of Encinitas, amenities for this hotel include hot breakfast buffet, free high speed internet, pool, in room refrigerator and microwave, and a complimentary USA Today newspaper. Pet friendly rooms are available

Inns of America Suites   5010 Avenida Encinas
Carlsbad, CA
(760) 929-8200

This motel is located a short walk from the beach and is just minutes from Legoland and The Flower Fields. Amenities include deluxe continental breakfast, pool, and exercise facility.

La Quinta Inn San Diego Carlsbad   760 Macadamia Drive
Carlsbad, CA
(760) 438-2828

This motel is located less than 4.5 miles from Legoland and near South Ponto State Beach. Downtown Carlsbad with shopping and restaurants is close by. There is a shopping center with grocery store, fast food restaurants, and other amenities one block away. Motel amenities include free Wi-Fi, continental breakfast, in room microwave and refrigerator, and an outdoor pool. Apparently pets are welcome. Contact the La Quinta for more information.

The West Inn and Suites

4970 Avenida Encinas
Carlsbad, CA
(760) 448-4500

The West Inn and Suites has been highly rated by visitors to internet travel websites. It is within walking distance to Carlsbad beaches and just a short drive down the street from the Legoland entrance. Amenities include complimentary breakfast, free underground parking, microwaves, refrigerators, dog and cat friendly rooms, complementary shuttle service, fitness center, outdoor pool with Jacuzzi, and free Wi-Fi.

C. Other Lodging

Beach Terrace Inn Carlsbad

2775 Ocean St
Carlsbad, CA
(760) 729-5951

This hotel is located directly on the beach. It offers studio suites, ocean view suites, and grand guestrooms with two queen sized beds. Amenities include a pool overlooking the beach, beach towels, direct beach access, ocean views from some rooms, and continental breakfast.

Best Western Beach View Lodge

3180 Carlsbad Blvd.
Carlsbad, CA
(760) 729-1151

This hotel, located in Carlsbad, offers six deluxe bedroom suites in addition to 41 newly renovated standard and deluxe guestrooms. Amenities include a courtyard heated swimming pool and whirlpool spa.

Courtyard by Marriot Carlsbad

5835 Owens Avenue
Carlsbad, CA
(760) 431-9399

This newly renovated hotel is located in Carlsbad's business district, but is close to local beaches, The Flower Fields, Carlsbad Premium Outlets, and Legoland. Amenities include high speed internet, fitness center, heated outdoor pool, and whirlpool. The Courtyard Café serves breakfast on site.

Four Seasons Aviara

7100 Four Seasons Point
Carlsbad, CA
(760) 603-6800

This elegant resort is located close to Legoland. The Four Seasons Aviara has kid friendly amenities that include a family pool and water play area, life sized tepee, game room as well as bedtime milk and cookies for young guests the night of your arrival. In room amenities include Play

Stations, complimentary use of the hotel's children's DVD library, childproofing supplies, cribs and roll-aways, and complimentary infant furnishings such as strollers and high chairs. Have a child three or under? Upon request your room will also be outfitted with diapers and wipes, bumper guards on the coffee table and end table, baby shampoo and wash, bathtub spout covers shaped like soft plastic animals, and swim diapers for the wading pool! Other amenities offered are: complimentary newspaper, thick terry robes, wired or wireless internet access, and twice daily housekeeping service. A surf concierge and beach butler are some of the more creative amenities offered by this top notch property.

The Four Seasons offers a Legoland adventure package. See http://www.fourseasons.com/aviara/rates_and_reservations.html for more details.

Hilton Garden Inn Carlsbad

6450 Carlsbad Blvd
Carlsbad, CA
(760) 476-0800

This is a beautiful hotel with a great location, just across the street from Carlsbad State Beach. Amenities include refrigerator/microwave, complimentary shuttle service within five miles (This includes Legoland), exercise facility, pool and whirlpool, cribs, high chairs, playpens, complimentary USA Today Newspaper and complimentary internet access. There is a restaurant on site and many restaurants within shuttle distance.

La Costa Resort and Spa

2100 Costa del Mar Road
Carlsbad, CA
(800) 854-5000
(760) 438-9111

This luxury resort has seven amazing swimming pools that include three water slides and a sandy beach pool as well as a game room for the kids. Other amenities include complimentary cribs, childproofing supplies upon request, stroller rentals, organized kids activities, an arrival goody bag, infant supplies (including diaper genies play pens, and high chairs), complimentary newspaper, Nintendo game cubes and Game Boys are available upon request. There is also a golf course and an on-site spa and fitness center. Prices are steep and include a resort fee, but if you are interested in a luxurious family getaway this may be the place for you!

Ramada Carlsbad by the Sea	751 Macadamia Dr. Carlsbad, CA (800) 644-9394 (760) 438-2285

Ramada Carlsbad by the Sea is located close to Interstate 5. Amenities include 27″ televisions, cable, refrigerators, microwaves, pay-per-view movies, Nintendo, continental hot breakfast buffet, a large heated pool and a Jacuzzi. The Ramada Carlsbad by the Sea also offers suites with fully equipped kitchens. A shopping center with supermarket, pharmacy, dry cleaner, and various restaurants is two blocks from this hotel.

Residence Inn San Diego Carlsbad	2000 Faraday Ave Carlsbad, CA (760) 431-9999

Located just one mile from Legoland, this hotel provides suites equipped with refrigerator, microwave, etc. The Residence Inn also offers cribs, a breakfast buffet and social hour, a pool, and a fitness center.

D.   *Camping*

Traveling on a budget or just want to camp on the beach? The South Carlsbad State Beach campground is only two freeway exits away from Legoland. The campsite features 222 RV/Tent Camping sites. The campground has token operated showers so bring some change. Like most state beach campgrounds in California, it fills up fast! Try to reserve your spot as early as possible and have a backup plan in case they are full. San Elijo State Beach Campground in Encinitas is also a popular choice for families. When camping on the coast, pack warm clothes. When the fog rolls in or sometimes stays all day it can be very chilly

V.   What to bring

A.   *Food*

Legoland's official policy states that outside food is not allowed in the park, except for infants and individuals with medical reasons. Even so most of my friends are Legoland pass holders, and none of us have ever been approached by the Legoland staff for bringing outside food. In order to avoid the high cost of food, I usually bring snacks and water bottles and sometimes a picnic lunch or dinner. This really cuts down on the cost of our visit, and ensures that we can visit frequently. I must admit that we do sometimes purchase some granny apple fries to share as a family. They are one of the best desserts in Legoland!

What I would recommend:

❋ Don't bring a cooler. If you need to use a cooler, have a tail gate party or eat on the grass as you approach the entrance to the park.

❋ Do bring food in a soft sided lunch box concealed in a backpack or in a stroller. Non perishable snacks, water bottles, and juice boxes are also great. When I am traveling light with my 9 year-old and his friend I sometimes just stuff my pockets or a fanny pack with fruit leather or granola bars.

❋ Don't make your picnic too obvious. Eat at one of the many benches around the park or on the outskirts of a food area, if it is not overly busy.

❋ If you have any problems with the Legoland staff, get your hand stamped and have a picnic on the grassy approach to the park.

B.   *Swimsuit, Towel, and Sunscreen*

One thing that you should know about Legoland is you may get wet! Both the Explore Village and Pirate Shores areas have water rides or attractions where both participants and bystanders may get wet. If you have the space, I would definitely pack a swimsuit and a light towel for each kid. You will be doing a lot of walking, but water resistant shoes or sandals do come in handy in these areas.

Lockers are available for $2.00 per use next to Pirate Shores. This is a good investment if you have any valuable that you would not feel comfortable leaving in your stroller or backpack. The lockers are hard to find. Look for them at the bathrooms between Pirate Shores (#43 on Legoland map) and the Wildwoods Miniature Golf Course (#11). The lockers are located on the side of the building next to the Women's bathroom.

C.   Sweatshirt

Many Carlsbad days start out foggy and cool, get warm as the sun comes out, then cool down again as the ocean breezes begin to blow. If you tend to get chilly pack a sweatshirt. If there is a chance of rain, a raincoat will come in handy. There are lots of fun things to do indoors at Legoland, but they are spaced far apart.

D.   Comfortable Shoes

Legoland is a big park and lacks any kind of tram or shuttle to get you around the park. Make sure that you wear comfortable shoes. You will be doing a lot of walking!

E.   Stroller

For families with kids under 4 or 5 years of age, a stroller can be a real lifesaver. The park is very big and there is a lot of ground to cover. In case of a meltdown it may be advisable to make a quick wheeled exit! Strollers are also great ways to tote all the gear necessary for a truly fun day at Legoland. Stroller parking is seldom a problem, and there are few areas that don't permit strollers. You will, however, need to scope out the stroller routes in and out of Miniland since they are kind of hidden. Some families bring wagons in lieu of strollers.

If you can't bring your own stroller, you can rent one at the Marketplace at the front of the park. They have single, double, infant, and whimsical vehicle strollers available for rent at reasonable prices.

Strollers	Daily Rate	Deposit
Single	$7.00	$2.00
Double	$13.00	$2.00
Infant	$7.00	$2.00
Whimsical Vehicle	$8.00	$2.00

If you bring a stroller, then decide that you don't want to use it to get around the park, you can check it at Member Services.

 If you happen to need an air pump to fill up your pneumatic tires on your stroller, Guest Services has a compressor. Just ask for it.

F.   *Wheelchair*

This park is big. If there are members of your party that are elderly or disabled, they may want to consider a wheelchair rental.

Manual and electric wheelchairs are available for rent at the Marketplace. The manual wheelchairs are heavy, so bring a strong person along to do the pushing!

Manual wheelchairs cost $10 + $2.00 deposit. Electric wheelchairs cost $35 + $2 deposit.

Most of the rides are disabled accessible. Pick up a brochure at Guest Services that outlines Legoland's access in detail.

VI. Getting There and Parking

A. *Directions to Legoland.*

Legoland California's address is:
One Legoland Drive
Carlsbad, CA 92008

Directions: From Interstate 5 – Exit Cannon Road in Carlsbad. Go east and follow the signs to Legoland Drive.

B. *Taking the Train / Public Transportation*

Both Amtrak, Los Angeles Metrolink and the San Diego Coaster trains drop riders off close to Legoland.

If you are taking Amtrak or Metrolink get off at the Oceanside station. Legoland is about 7.5 miles away. You could take a cab or transfer to the Coaster train and then take the bus.

If you are arriving by Coaster train you can get off at the Carlsbad Village or Carlsbad Poinsettia Station. From these locations Legoland is just a short taxi ride away. From Carlsbad Village you can take the NCTD bus route 321 that stops right in front of Legoland.

It may also be possible to use the train if you are staying in a hotel near Legoland. Many local hotels have shuttles to the train station.

C. *Drop Off & Pick Up Area*

If someone is dropping your family off at Legoland, there is a convenient drop off and pick up area just before you reach the parking kiosks. The drop off area is a pull out on your left. Look for the giant Lego welcome sign.

D.   *Parking*

Hours

The Legoland parking lot opens at 8:30 am. There is no charge for parking the last hour of the day.

Parking Prices

Legoland parking charges are as follows:

$5	Motorcycles
$10	Cars
$20	Preferred Parking

Re-entry is available with a valid parking stub during the same day of visit.

RV Parking

$11   Campers/RV's (Overnight RV Parking is not permitted).

Follow the signs upon entering the park. RV parking is on the far side of the parking lot. The lot is located just to the right of the entrance at the front of the parking lot and is a great location. It is definitely not a problem to drive an RV to Legoland or pull your trailer with you.

Disabled Parking

Disabled spaces are available close to the entrance. A disabled placard is required.

Preferred Parking

In order to park in the closest parking lot to the entrance you must pay a $20.00 parking fee. Is it worth it? If someone in your party has limited mobility with no disabled placard, this may be a better option. If not, unless it is a very crowded day and you really want to park close, I would not recommend preferred parking. There are lots of parking strategies that will get you almost as close for half the price.

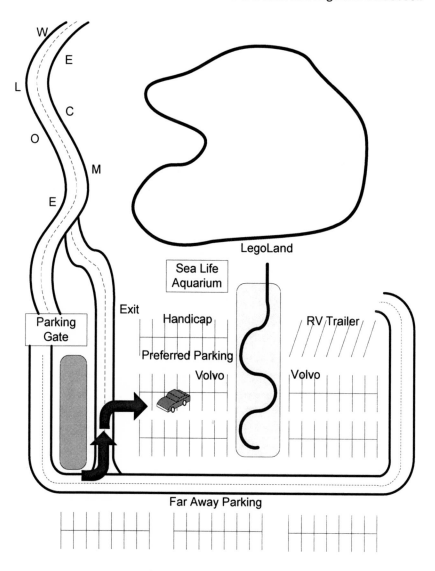

Figure 1 - Legoland Parking Map

Close in Parking (Dad's Secret)

As you enter the park, turn left where it says disabled and preferred parking. The top parking lot is for disabled and preferred parking only. The parking lot just below this is for everyone and is seldom crowded because people read the signs and think there is no parking for the general public.

Other Parking Strategies

If the first parking row is full, continue to the lowest parking lot on the left or the large parking area to the right of the entrance. The strategy in these lots is to park as close as possible to the center walkway that goes to the park. Even if you have to park in one of the rows further down, you will still save some steps. This can be crucial when you are escorting a grouchy toddler from the park.

Volvo Parking

If you have a Volvo, take your reserved spot in the top center rows of the parking lot. No kidding! Volvo is a corporate sponsor of Legoland. So pay your parking fee, but when you get to the lot, look for a Volvo Reserved Spots close to the front entrance. There are almost always a few available any time of day.

VII. The Park

A.   *General Approach*

Things tend to get more crowded at "The Beginning," then thin out by the time you reach Fun Town at the back of the park. If you are visiting with preschool age kids turn left (west) upon entering the park and start with Dino Island. Most of the rides on the left side of the park tend to be geared toward a younger crowd. If you have school age kids head right (east). Most visitors to the park do not use this route, but the right side of the park has more activities that are appropriate for older kids, and you'll also find it is less crowded.

Another way to avoid the crowds at opening would be to start your day by walking through Miniland, and coming out by Castle Hill. You will be enjoying the middle of the park as others are making their way from the front. Some rides don't open until 10:30 am, but there are plenty of opportunities for fun open at 10 am.

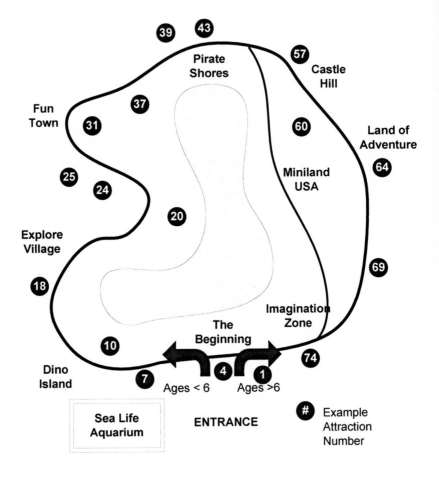

Figure 2 – Diagram of Legoland.
Be sure to pick up a color map when entering Legoland at the ticket turn styles.
The attraction numbers in this guidebook match the ones on the Legoland map.

B.   *The Beginning*

The Big Shop (#4) – This shop as its name suggests contains the largest selection of Lego and Legoland merchandise in the country. It gets very busy, so be prepared to keep your little one close

The Market (#6) – This market has snacks, fresh pastries and Danishes, light sandwiches, etc.   Check out the coffee special, $9.50 for an insulated cup with unlimited refills.

Marketplace/Stroller & Wheelchair Rental (#5) – Here is where guests can rent strollers as well as electric or manual wheelchairs.

 Please note stroller and wheelchair rentals are on a first-come, first-served basis.

The Market Place stocks film, sundries, and assorted Lego souvenirs. If you are leaving the park and want to avoid the crowds at the Big Shop, you might want to check it out.

Package Pickup (#5) – Legoland gives families the option to shop early and pick up purchases as they exit the Park.

Kodak Photo Center (#3) – You can pick up any of the photos taken of your family by Legoland staff here.

Guest Services / Lost Parents (#2) – This area provides membership renewal assistance and other services. Step into the Membership area and pick up a free Lego magazine if you are not already a subscriber. A pump that can be used to inflate stroller tires is also available at this location.

First Aid (#1) – Guests use this area for breast-feeding infants, using electrical outlets for medical appliances and basic first aid needs.

VIII. Rides, Attractions and Shows

Icon Key

Ride Attraction

$ Additional Fee Charged

Show or theater experience

Interactive Play Area

Swim suits recommended – Water activity.

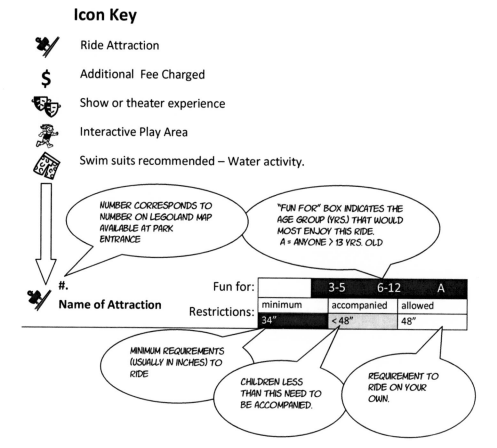

NUMBER CORRESPONDS TO NUMBER ON LEGOLAND MAP AVAILABLE AT PARK ENTRANCE

"FUN FOR" BOX INDICATES THE AGE GROUP (YRS.) THAT WOULD MOST ENJOY THIS RIDE.
A = ANYONE > 13 YRS. OLD

#.
Name of Attraction

Fun for:	3-5	6-12	A
Restrictions:	minimum	accompanied	allowed
	34"	< 48"	48"

MINIMUM REQUIREMENTS (USUALLY IN INCHES) TO RIDE

CHILDREN LESS THAN THIS NEED TO BE ACCOMPANIED.

REQUIREMENT TO RIDE ON YOUR OWN.

A.   Dino Island

Check out the life sized Lego Dinosaurs!

7.
Coastersaurus

Fun for:		3-5	6-12	A
Restrictions:	minimum	accompanied		allowed
	34"	< 48"		48"

This is a perfect first roller coaster, but may lack some thrills for the older crowd. The first drop does a 360 that's pretty fun, but the rest of the ride is a lot of bouncy up and down then just a return back. As one of 3 roller coasters at the park, it's worth a ride. If the line is long, come back later. The end of the day is a great time to ride this ride.

8.
Dig Those Dinos

Fun for:	< 3	3-5	
Restrictions:	minimum	accompanied	allowed
	none		

This is a giant sand pit with concrete bones that kids can unearth by digging. My kids have fun there. It's a great thing to do with little kids while the big ones ride the roller coaster. You can rent a bucket and a shovel, but usually we just dig with our hands. Once you turn in your bucket and shovel you will receive a prize. At the time of my last visit it was a Lego paleontologist.

9.
$ Raptor Splash

Fun for:		6-12	A
Restrictions:	minimum	accompanied	allowed
	none		

Water balloon catapults for the entire family. Raptor Splash would be a welcome relief on a hot day. This attraction is seasonal and it charges an additional fee.

B. *Explore Village*

Lots of fun for younger kids!

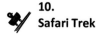

10.
Safari Trek

Fun for:	< 3	3-5	6-12	
Restrictions:	minimum	accompanied	allowed
	34"	< 48"	48"

Spot Lego animals on a whimsical jeep safari. My kids love this ride. Be aware kids less than 48 inches must be accompanied by an adult. The line for this ride can get long, but there is a Duplo play area to keep the kids busy. The signs indicating the line wait times are accurate. If the line is long you can wait more than 60 minutes for this ride.

11.
Fairy Tale Brook

Fun for:	< 3	3-5		
Restrictions:	minimum	accompanied	allowed
	none	< 48"	

Take a sweet boat ride through a Lego world populated by many of your child's favorite story book characters. Be aware that the line for this ride moves pretty slowly. If it is long, you might want to pass and return later. This ride provides a quiet break and is good for small children. If you are looking for an exciting ride, go somewhere else!

13.
Playtown Theater

Fun for:	< 3	3-5		
Restrictions:	minimum	accompanied	allowed
	none		

Playtown Theater is a real theater that gets dark and there is music and a few lighting special effects. Keep that in mind when deciding whether to take a very small child.

Journey to the Lost Temple is Legoland's first year round musical adventure comedy. The show was designed for kids age 2-12, but my timid 4 year-old found it to be a little loud and scary. Like many Legoland attractions, this show was both interactive and fun. Even my 9 year-old enjoyed it because it was funny.

Kids from the audience get to come up on stage and take part in the show. If your child volunteers, make sure that he or she is not prone to stage fright. The kids don't just stand there. They dance like an Egyptian or make a snake puppet slither.

The jokes are corny. The dialogue is somewhat cheesy. The music consists of pop songs from the 70's and 80's. Still this show is campy fun for the whole family. Check it out!

15. Water Works Magical Fountain	Fun for:	< 3	3-5	
	Restrictions:	minimum	accompanied	allowed
		none		

Water Works Magical Fountain is an interactive water play area where kids can play and splash to the tune of music! The water areas include Zany Zoo, Rain Maker and Musical Fountain. This is a fun place for people watching. There are plenty of benches were you can relax, have a snack, and keep an eye on the kids.

- ✳ At **Zany Zoo** kids pedal a bicycle, and pump to make the fountain work. Preschoolers and younger school age visitors really enjoy this activity
- ✳ At **Rain Maker** kids turn the crank to drench a Lego friend.
- ✳ Seen the movie Big? Adults and kids jump from dot to dot at the **Musical Fountain** creating a wonderful Lego Symphony.

15. Water Works Stomp and Spritz	Fun for:	< 3	3-5	
	Restrictions:	minimum	accompanied	allowed
		none		

Jets of water stream up, as the kids stomp on the fountain. This attraction is not always open, but can be a lot of fun. I have even spotted teenagers playing on it. The Pirate Shores Area (see page 63) can get you a lot wetter. Still if Pirate Shores is crowded or overwhelming for your little ones, this great place to cool off on a hot day. There are even giant driers to help dry you off after getting soaked!

16. Village Theater	Fun for:	< 3	3-5	6-12	A
	Restrictions:	minimum	accompanied	allowed	
		none			

Outdoor amphitheater used for special events.

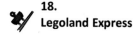

17. Duplo Playtown	Fun for:	< 3	3-5		
	Restrictions:	minimum	accompanied	allowed	
		none			

This is a really fun play area. Local moms bring their kids to play on a weekly basis. There are lots of slides to go down and pretend vehicles to drive. Your child can even put his little brother in a Lego jail! Sometimes in the summer there is water play. It's fun to hit this area when the park opens if you have preschoolers. It gets very busy later in the day. Do keep an eye on the little ones. There are lots of escape routes.

There are also some pavilions with Duplo blocks where mom and dad can take a rest and chat while the kids play. There is also a preschooler appropriate crawl through maze.

This area is supposed to be for kids 5-and-under, but I have taken 6 and 9 year-olds there and they have a great time. As long as the big kids are being respectful of the younger visitors, it is a place where the whole family can have fun.

18. Legoland Express	Fun for:	< 3	3-5		
	Restrictions:	minimum	accompanied	allowed	
		none	< 36"	36"	

This is a favorite ride for 4 year-old Destiny and 3 year-old Jared. They can ride this little train by themselves or accompanied by an adult. I love the mix of real California crops and Lego brick produce. Make sure to point out the artichokes and fresh strawberries.

C.   *Fun Town*

19. Kid Power Towers

Fun for:		3-5	6-12	A
Restrictions:		minimum	Accompanied	allowed
		40"	< 48"	48"

Get ready for some exercise. Kids and parents pull themselves up a rope then freefall down. This is the highest point in Legoland and a great way to get a view of the park and the ocean. *This ride opens at 10:30 am.*

20. Sky Cruiser

Fun for:		3-5	6-12	A
Restrictions:		minimum	Accompanied	allowed
		34"	< 48"	48"

This ride is not scary for the little ones, and the fact that the kids do the pedaling makes it fun for older ones as well. The line for this ride is long at peak times. There is a Duplo play area for the kids to play in while you wait, but the wait can still seem long for everyone. The general consensus from recent Legoland visitors is that the line may not be worth the wait. Think twice if it looks too busy. Try to hit this ride at an off peak time. The kids have fun pedaling to make this ride "go", but pedaling is not required to make the ride move. This is a great way to get an overview of the park as it circles the highest point in Legoland. *Note: This ride opens at 10:30 am.*

21. Sky Patrol

Fun for:	< 3	3-5	
Restrictions:	minimum	accompanied	allowed
	34"	< 48"	48"

Helicopters go up and down and spin around. This is a good activity to keep your under 3 year-old busy with a parent while the older kids enjoy the Volvo Driving School experiences. Every child must be accompanied by an adult and the helicopters only hold 2 riders. Next to the Sky Patrol are some fun stationary Lego shaped cars. These can provide a similar distraction.

24.	Fun for:		3-5	
Volvo Junior Driving School	Restrictions:	minimum	accompanied	allowed
		3 yrs."		5 yrs max

This is the little kid version of the Volvo driving school. Be aware that the ride operator will ask your child for his or her age. You can't sneak a 2 year-old on this ride! The ride operator will ask your child (not you!) for his or her age. Prepare to be embarrassed if you try to sneak your not quite 3 year-old on.

Your child will need to push the pedal on the car and do a little steering. My 3 year-old lacks the coordination to steer and accelerate the car, so he usually ends up being stuck or crashing several times during the ride. For the more coordinated little kids however, this ride is a great rite of passage. At the end of the ride your child will receive an official Legoland driver's license. You can pay $5 to have your picture taken and have it turned into a personalized license at the kiosk by the driving areas. You can also just take the drivers license home, fill in your info, and add your own picture.

25.	Fun for:			6-12
Volvo Driving School	Restrictions:	minimum	accompanied	allowed
		6 yrs.		13 yrs. max

Kids love this ride! They get to drive electric cars. There are real traffic signals and stop signs. The line may get long, but is worth the wait. Since large groups of kids participate at one time, the line goes fast. At the end of the ride your child will receive an official Legoland driver's license. You can pay $5 to have your picture taken and have it turned into a personalized license at the kiosk by the driving areas. You can also just take the drivers license home, fill in your info, and add your own picture.

Keep your camera trained on your young driver, because there are some great opportunities for photo-ops. If the line for this ride is short, take advantage and get on as soon as you can. This is one of the best rides for kids at Legoland.

26.
Fun Town Stage

Fun for:	< 3	3-5	6-12	A
Restrictions:	Minimum	accompanied	allowed	
	None			

This is a fun silly show **"The Big Test"** that teaches fire safety. Inexperienced firefighters learn to work together as a team in order to fight fires. You will be singing "put the wet stuff on the hot stuff" long after you leave the amphitheater. This is great place to take a break and enjoy some interactive fun. Don't sit in the first few rows of this theater if you want to stay dry.

31.
Fun Town Fire Academy

Fun for:	< 3	3-5	6-12	A
Restrictions:	Minimum	accompanied	allowed	
	34"	< 48"	48"	

This is a fun and exhausting ride for the whole family. You will really get your exercise. The "drivers" make the engine go, by pumping levers up and down. When you reach the structure on fire, two "fire fighters" get out and pump water to put out the fire. There are two sides to this attraction. However, at off peak times only one side may be open. The South side has pumps, which require a lot of adult effort. The north side is much easier. You push a button to make the water squirt. Once the fire disappears, you jump back in the engine and race to where you started. The object is to be the first family back. This ride has a maximum of four riders. It takes a lot of effort, so I would recommend having at least two adults or big kids to get the truck moving and put out the fire. The little guys enjoy going along for the ride. *Note: This ride opens at 10:30 am.*

32.
Lego Factory Tour

Fun for:		3-5	6-12	A
Restrictions:	Minimum	accompanied	allowed	
	None			

Ever wanted to see how Lego bricks are made? Here's your chance. You start out your tour with a cute movie about Lego creation, then walk through and watch a Lego brick being made in the factory. Check out the vintage Lego sets at the end of your tour. It is fun to see how Lego bricks have evolved.

Keep a look out for freebees at the end of the tour. We have picked up back issues of Lego magazine and trading cards. Your tour comes out at the Lego Club House. This is a store, so you may be saying no a lot, but you can buy some really fun Lego bricks in bulk. At the back of the store is a play area with lots of tiny big kid Lego bricks. This is a fun place to hang out with older kids, although my son mourns the absence of mini figs (Lego people).

33.
Skyscraper Climb

Fun for:			6-12	A
Restrictions:	minimum	accompanied	allowed
	none		

This is your standard climbing wall activity. It is not always open, so take a look before you make any promises to your young adventurer. One climb is $6. Two climbs are $10.

34.
Adventurers' Club

Fun for:	< 3	3-5	6-12	A
Restrictions:	minimum	accompanied	allowed
	none		

My school age son loves the Adventurers' Club. My preschoolers find it a little scary. The atmosphere is reminiscent of Indiana Jones. You search for keys hidden in the Amazon rainforest, ancient Egypt, and the Arctic Lego brick worlds! Be prepared to exit into the front of the store. Hopefully you can sneak the kids out without having to buy anything!

36.
Flight Squadron

Fun for:	< 3	3-5	
Restrictions:	minimum	accompanied	allowed
	34"	< 48"	48"

This biplane ride is located by Pirate Shores. Kids under 48 inches need to be accompanied by an adult. If you are the parent riding along, note that the planes are tricky to get into, and you have to maneuver your legs down into the nose cone of the plane. My mom really banged her knee up trying to get into the plane. If you are not feeling limber, the Cargo Ace Ride in the Land of Adventure area might be more fun for everyone. *Note: This ride opens at 10:30 am.*

37.
Skipper School

Fun for:	< 3	3-5	6-12	A
Restrictions:	Minimum	accompanied	allowed	
	34"	< 48"	48"	

This a fun adventure for the whole family. The boats seat two, and the driver navigates around the lake. There is a little bit of skill involved at some point, so if your little guy is driving, be prepared to take the wheel from time to time. Also be careful entering and exiting the boat. My cell phone fell in the water as I was getting out of our boat. Legoland staff cheerfully fished it out for me. There is a Duplo play area in case the line is long. *Note: This ride opens at 10:30 am.*

D.   *Pirate Shores*

This is one of the most fun areas at Legoland and a great place for parents to take a break. There is only one entrance into the area, so you can keep an eye on the kids. Any kid who loves water play will want to stay there for hours. Separate areas for little and big kids make it ideal for almost any age group. Family restrooms located across from Garden Restaurant are available for changing. Lockers are available at this location for a current price of $2 per use. Bring some quarters!

Make sure you bring bathing suits and towels. Water shoes or flip flops would also be great. I have seen some very soggy socks. These necessities are sold at a shop located in Pirate Shores, but the price is premium ($15 dollars for a kids swim suit).

There is a nice slope covered with artificial grass so spread out a towel and watch the kids at Swabbies Deck. If you are keeping an eye on a big guy, there are benches to your left as you approach Soak-N-Sail. A pirate band made out of Lego bricks welcomes you at the entrance to the Pirate Shores area. The bench surrounding this lively crew is also a good place to sit and keep an eye on the action. The first time our family visited this attraction my husband and I had lunch on the bench while the children played. It was like a date!

Be aware that outside of the benches or slope seating area you will get wet. The kids do not hesitate to squirt unsuspecting grownups. If you plan to be chasing your kid around either play area I would recommend a swimsuit. If you plan to be a bystander, water resistant shoes and clothes that dry off quickly still might come in handy.

Pirate Shores is not open at certain times of year and is subject to closure during cold and inclement weather. Sometimes Soak-N-Sail is closed and Swabbies Deck is open. If you are looking forward to this chapter of your Legoland adventure you might want to call ahead to see what attractions will be open.

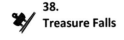

	38.	Fun for:		**3-5**	**6-12**	
	Treasure Falls	Restrictions:	minimum	accompanied	allowed	
			36" & 4 yrs	< 48"	48"	

This mini flume ride drops you twelve feet. The big kids in your party may find it underwhelming, but little guys may get a thrill. Whimsical Lego monkeys and pirates make this ride more enjoyable.

	39.	Fun for:		**3-5**	**6-12**	**A**
	Soak-N-Sail	Restrictions:	minimum	accompanied	allowed	
			36" for slides			

This big kid water play area is really a blast. There is a giant climbing structure filled with assorted water cannons and slides. There is even a giant bucket that periodically dumps 300 gallons of water. You know it's coming when the bell starts ringing. If you don't want to get wet get out of the way. A swim suit, towel, and change of clothes are must have items for this attraction. Swim diapers are required for all children under 4 years of age.

Dads will enjoy using the assorted water cannons, squirters, and buckets that soak the ever cheerful Legoland staff. Also from the second story facing the Splash Battle Ride you can squirt Splash Battle riders.

Soak and Sail may be appropriate for brave 4-5 year-olds, but other little guys may be intimidated by the large amount of water and kids.

This ride gets very crowded in the heat of the day. It is best to visit this area as soon as the fog burns off or at the lunch hour. That way you can have fun getting wet and dry off by afternoon. This ride is seasonal and may be closed in colder weather

	40.	Fun for:	**< 3**	**3-5**		
	Swabbies Deck	Restrictions:	minimum	accompanied	allowed	
			none			

This area is ideal for preschoolers. There are plenty of spray jets and water fountains to jump on. Destiny and Jared my little ones love to ride on the big puppy and kitten statues. There are swings that are subject to gentle squirts of water which make them ideal for pre-walkers. My 3 year-old loves to lie down in a water puddle and take a break. There are also lots of levers to be pumped that make the water squirt. This is an exciting interactive area to play in on a hot day. Be sure to wear a swimsuit and bring a towel. Swim diapers are required for kids under 4.

41. Captain Cranky's Challenge	Fun for:		3-5	6-12	
	Restrictions:	minimum	accompanied	allowed	
		36"	< 42"	42"	

This giant pirate ship rocks back and forth and spins in circles. This simple ride would be a thrill for young school age kids. If you are looking for maximum excitement, try to sit at the ends of the ship.

42. Buccaneer's Booty	Fun for:		3-5	6-12	A
	Restrictions:	minimum	accompanied	allowed	
		none			

Forget your swimsuit? Need a temporary tattoo? In the market for a foam rubber pirate sword? This store has you covered. Be prepared for high prices.

43. Splash Battle	Fun for:		3-5	6-12	A
	Restrictions:	minimum	accompanied	allowed	
		36"	< 44"	44"	

This is a great pirate themed boat ride. As you enter the ride you are in

range of various water cannons. Look at the ground. If it's wet you're in range. There are also water cannons along the Splash Battle route that shoot the riders. These are very popular. A well coordinated team working in unison directing its water spray at a rider can get them pretty wet. The fun part is that riders also get to squirt water cannons at other boats and at passers by as you move along. Be prepared to get wet since the other boats will try to squirt you. There are also lots of Lego pirate scenes to enjoy. Little guys who don't like getting wet should avoid this ride! Depending on the aim of your fellow sailors you may get pretty soaked.

Dad's Shooting Strategies: The key to the water cannons on the boats is that they have stops preventing them from rotating all the way. However, the cannons on the left of the boat can shoot to the right side and the cannons on the right of the boat shoot to the left. Once you know this you have a chance.

Beware of the streams of water coming from the walkway. You can get very wet on this ride, especially if the shore gunners have read the strategy below. Some people buy plastic rain ponchos to wear.

 Dad's Shooting Strategies: One of the best parts of this ride is to man one of the shore water cannons hidden behind the fences. These cannons seem to have an advantage over the ones on the ship. To be most effective communicate with your fellow gunners and pick a single rider per ship to target.

E.   Castle Hill

This is one of my favorite areas of Legoland. It hosts a great play area and fun rides and activities for every age group and is home to the famous *Granny Apple Fries*, my favorite Legoland treat. Castle Hill also hosts annual Brick or Treat festivities at Halloween.

$

45.	Fun for:		**3-5**	**6-12**	**A**
Wild Woods Golf	Restrictions:	minimum	accompanied		allowed
		none			

Miniature Golf Legoland style! Kids 3 to 100 would enjoy this attraction. The golf course is pretty easy without a lot of traps or obstacles. At every turn you will encounter cute Lego woodland animals. This attraction is an extra charge. If you buy your Legoland ticket from Costco, you get a free round of golf.

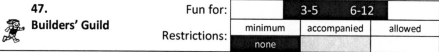

46.	Fun for:	**< 3**	**3-5**		
Enchanted Walk	Restrictions:	minimum	accompanied		allowed
		none			

My little ones enjoy this quiet woodland walk. There are Lego forest animals to discover around every turn. Plenty of benches make this a great place for a picnic or a rest. The path way is stroller friendly.

47.	Fun for:		**3-5**	**6-12**	
Builders' Guild	Restrictions:	minimum	accompanied		allowed
		none			

This Lego Pavilion just past the Enchanted Walk is a great place to take a break with your Lego fan. My 9 year-old wishes there were Lego figures, but you can still build a lot of great contraptions or add to the Lego Castle at the center of the Builder's Guild. This is a good place to eat your lunch, since the grownups can keep eating and talking long after the kids have moved on to Lego brick construction. Since this is tucked away from the main area of Knight's Kingdom it doesn't tend to be crowded.

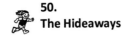

50.
The Hideaways

Fun for:		3-5	6-12	A
Restrictions:	minimum	accompanied		allowed
	none			

This is one of the best places to get a lot of energy out. Kids can climb, slide and wiggle through a variety of obstacles. Brave 3 year-olds and 4 year-olds would enjoy this ride with adult supervision. Some little ones may be intimidated by the crush of big kids having fun. Still, this can be a great place to bring a wide age range of children and there is no waiting in line so it is a top pick for both parents and kids.

You can do everyone a favor by reminding your children that they must only go down the slides and up the climbing structures. Ask them to watch out for younger kids who may not take kindly to being bopped by hanging punching bags and the like.

It is very easy to lose a kid here. In fact it is almost a given. Luckily the entrance to the Hideaways is also the exit so you can stake out a spot near by and make sure you catch your little one before he or she can escape. Don't plan to see your kids anytime soon however, this area is so engaging it may be a while before they are wiling to leave. Bring a snack or a cup of coffee and plan to stay a while. Get acquainted with moms and dads who are sitting around you.

51.
King's Treasury

Fun for:		3-5	6-12	
Restrictions:	minimum	accompanied		allowed
	none			

Kids get to pan for minerals. These would make a fun souvenir. There is an extra charge for this attraction.

53.
Courtyard Theater

Fun for:		3-5	6-12	A
Restrictions:	minimum	accompanied		allowed
	none			

This stage sometimes hosts a pirate show during the summer months. It uses simple special effects and lots of humor. If you are in the area the show might be worth catching.

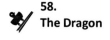

55.
The Royal Joust

Fun for:		3-5	
	minimum	accompanied	allowed
Restrictions:	36" & 4 yrs		12 yrs. & 170 lbs max.

Destiny and Jared, my preschoolers love this ride. They really don't enforce the minimum age limit to ride the horses so you can probably sneak on your mature 3 year-old. They are so proud that they get to ride all by themselves. Since only three kids go out at a time, the line can be brutal. Try to hit this at an off time. This is great ride for photo-ops. After you load the kids on the ride stake out a good spot to capture a picture of your knight or lady. *Note: This ride opens at 10:30 am.*

58.
The Dragon

Fun for:		3-5	6-12	A
	minimum	accompanied		allowed
Restrictions:	40"	< 48" w/ adult		48"

This is a fun roller coaster. It starts out as a simple ride into "the castle". There are lots of funny Lego castle scenes. Suddenly the roller coaster takes hold and you find yourself outside in a roller coaster that has some zip to it. It won't be number one your roller coaster fan's list, but there is a lot to enjoy about this indoor/outdoor attraction. Since the castle is somewhat dark, really little ones may be intimidated by the first part of the ride. The line for this ride can be long. If the line is just outside the castle, go ahead and take a ride. If the line winds through the grave yard be prepared for a long wait or come back later.

60.
Knights' Tournament

Fun for:			6-12	A
	minimum	accompanied		allowed
Restrictions:	40"	< 55"		6'4" & 220 lb. max

This is Justin's all time favorite ride. It is not for the faint hearted. I have never seen anything like it at another theme park. Giant Robotic arms like the one used in automotive assembly plants to weld on car doors spin you around and almost dip you into a slimy moat. Things you should know about this ride are:

You get to choose the intensity of the ride. Some levels go upside down; some levels are faster and jerkier than others. Be sure to inform your younger companions that this ride has very strict height specifications. Kids have to be pretty tall to ride the higher levels. Shorter kids may need to wear a safety vest and can only ride levels one or two.

Everything will fall out of your pockets. Make sure to leave your belongings in the cubby by the ride. This includes flip flops as well as earrings or facial piercings.

Spectators can use water cannons to blast large blasts of compressed air and moat water at you. Bring some quarters and dollar bills for the blasters. If you don't want to get wet wait in line for the East End. The blasters there have been removed.

 Dad's Shooting Strategies: *Practice on some folks before your party is on the ride. There is a delay on the cannons that you need to account for. With a little practice your party will get wet.*

Younger kids make the dragon "speak" while waiting for a big brother or sister to finish with the ride. Under the dragon there is a trumpet. Speak into it and your words are transformed into an evil dragon voice. There is also a throne by this ride. It's great for a photo-op or just playing king of the castle while you wait.

F. *Land of Adventure*

With the current Indiana Jones craze this area is sure to be a hit. It recreates 1920's Egypt in Lego bricks. There are rides for every age group, including a very fun ball play area. It's a small space, but very well utilized.

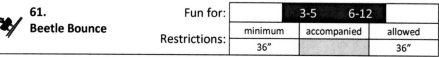

61.
Beetle Bounce

Fun for:		3-5	6-12	
Restrictions:	minimum	accompanied		allowed
	36"			36"

Beetle Bounce brings you to the top of a fifteen foot tower then drops you down. My 9 year-old really enjoyed this ride. He thought that it had a fast drop and wanted to go again after his first try.

63.
Cargo Ace

Fun for:	< 3	3-5		
Restrictions:	minimum	accompanied		allowed
	walking	<36"		36"

These are fun planes for little kids. I appreciated the fact that parents don't necessarily have to ride along in these single seated planes. That said, I did navigate for one of my kids and it was a comfortable ride. Make sure that grownups ride in the back seat. It has much more leg room! The planes go around and gently up and down. The end result lots of smiles and laughter.

64.
Lost Kingdom
Adventure

Fun for:		3-5	6-12	A
Restrictions:	minimum	accompanied		allowed
	34"	<42"		42"

Ride an all terrain roadster deep into dark ancient temple ruins. There are two people per seat and four people per car. Blast targets with laser guns in order to recover stolen treasure. Riders pass through 10 different areas including a spider's lair, professor's lab, mummy relics, and a skeleton band. A computer records every shot, so at the end you can compare scores with your riding companions. Fun details for this ride are the hood ornaments on each car constructed using Lego bricks.

This ride would only be appropriate for brave 3-5 year-olds. My 4 year-old found it to be too dark and noisy for her taste.

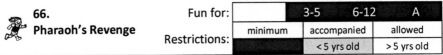

	Fun for:		3-5	6-12	A
66.					
Pharaoh's Revenge	Restrictions:	minimum	accompanied		allowed
			< 5 yrs old		> 5 yrs old

The name says it all. This compact two story attraction allows kids and parents to lob soft foam balls at friends and family. To reach the second story kids can use an outside climbing structure or climb the stairs inside. Pharaoh's Revenge is loud and crazy. Little ones must be accompanied by an adult. It is easy to sit on a bench outside and keep a close eye on the exit, so if your kids are old enough to enter the attraction alone this may be the way to go. On the other hand, if you have some pent up frustration to vent after a long day of hanging out with whiny kids, by all means let the battle begin!

G.   *Imagination Zone*

This area has some of the most fun hands on activities in Legoland, yet it is easy to overlook as you pass through on your way to the rides.   It also contains the Technic Test Track roller coaster, the only conventional "big kid" roller coaster at Legoland.

69.
Lego Technic Test Track

Fun for:		3-5	6-12	A
		minimum	accompanied	allowed
Restrictions:		42" & 4 yrs	< 48"	48"

This is a fun, fast roller coaster that goes 26 miles per hour with a five story drop. It is a bit jerky, but the school age crowd will find it thrilling. A very brave, tall 4 or 5 year-old might enjoy this ride, but it is a real big kid roller coaster so more timid preschoolers should avoid it.

Waiting in line can be pretty tedious despite the humorous videos that involve crash test dummies. Try to hit this ride when the line is short. It will seem much more fun.

67.
Aquazone Wave Racers

Fun for:		3-5	6-12	A
		minimum	accompanied	allowed
Restrictions:		40"	< 52"	52"

This zippy ride is lots of fun. You are standing on a Jet Ski type vehicle racing around in a circle at top speed. Spectators push a button, and compressed air comes out of the water and hits you with a water air blast. Plan to be damp, but not necessarily wet. Well, my shoes and pant legs got very wet.

71.
Lego Show Place

Fun for:		3-5	6-12	A
		minimum	accompanied	allowed
Restrictions:		none		

Spellbreaker: This 4-D movie adventure presents a whimsical Lego medieval tale of adventure. My 9 year-old loves it. My preschoolers were intimidated by the 4-D effects.

Lego Racers 4-D: This 4-D racing movie has lots of special effects. The general consensus is that Spellbreaker is a better movie, so if you have to choose, pass on this one.

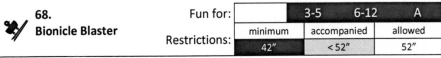

68. Bionicle Blaster	Fun for:		3-5	6-12	A
	Restrictions:	minimum	accompanied		allowed
		42"	< 52"		52"

The Teacup ride for Legoland. Very dizzy fun.

72. Bionicle Evolution	Fun for:		3-5	6-12	A
	Restrictions:	minimum	accompanied		allowed
		none			

Is your child a Bionicle fan? This area is Bionicle heaven! There are basins full of Bionicle pieces to build his or her own personal Bionicle. Original sketches from the comic books line the walls.

73. Maniac Challenge	Fun for:			6-12	A
	Restrictions:	minimum	accompanied		allowed
		none			

The Maniac Challenge offers 40 desktop personal computers loaded with Lego games like Bionicle, Drone Racers, Islands 2, Racers 2, Lego Friends, Chess and Soccer Mania. The kids love to try out Lego games based on their favorite characters, but there is also a fun, hands on activity available for parents and older Lego fans. At the entrance to this attraction, you can check out a number of sophisticated Lego brick sets. I do this every time. It is a very humbling experience for me as I try to follow the complex directions. The kids enjoy giving advice, and if all goes well you can be proud of your Lego building accomplishments. This is a fun area to hang out in with older kids. Little kids can help you build some of the simpler sets, but they do not have Duplo blocks at this location. This attraction may be closed on weekdays from 10 am – 2 pm due to Education Program classes.

74.	Fun for:			6-12	A
Lego Mindstorms	Restrictions:	minimum	accompanied		allowed
		10 yrs.			

This activity is exclusively for big kids. You have a chance to build and program computerized Lego Mindstorms robots. Mindstorms are really interesting Lego sets, part erector set part high tech robot. The Mindstorms activity requires kids to carefully listen to and follow directions. This activity is really fun and encourages problem solving. You will be amazed at what you kids can do. Make a reservation at the Mindstorms Building under Einstein's head as soon as you enter the park, since spots fill up early. Age requirements for this activity are: If accompanied by an adult age 9 or entering 3rd grade; if unaccompanied age 12 and up.

Be sure to sign up for a session as soon as you hit the park. It's not uncommon for the Mindstorms sessions to fill up on busy days by mid morning. Do this first thing.

76.	Fun for:	< 3	3-5	
Duplo Play	Restrictions:	minimum	accompanied	allowed
		none		

Imagine a large room filled with almost every kind of Duplo block ever made. I discovered this area after many months of Legoland adventures and wish I had known about it earlier. This activity has no lines. And is fun in any kind of weather. There are different areas with roads, castles, a giant Lego crane, etc. This area is mostly for the little guys, but my 9 year-old has spent some time there building a giant Duplo bridge in the construction area and constructing a tall tower. Duplo play is great place for parents to sit for a while and build with their kids.

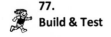

77.	Fun for:		3-5	6-12	A
Build & Test			minimum	accompanied	allowed
	Restrictions:		none		

This is also a really fun area. If you know what to ask for, you can keep every kid in your family happy for a while. At the main desk big kids check out a set of wheels with axles, then build vehicles with a wide assortment of big kid Lego bricks. There are a number of tracks with timers, and the kids can race their vehicles to see who has the fastest car. Little kids can also put a car together with a little help putting the wheels on a platform. Amazingly kids take turns at the track with minimal adult intervention. Still, if your child seems to be forgetting to give others a turn, a gentle reminder always helps.

You may be wondering if there are any activities for the under 5 set at this attraction. In addition to Lego activities around the walls of the room that adjoins the build and test area, parents can check out simple Dora the Explorer and castle Duplo sets that will keep the little guys busy while big brother or sister is racing.

This area is decorated with award winning designs from the Jr. Master Builder competitions that are held monthly in the park. These whimsical creations are sure to provide inspiration for your budding Lego engineer.

H.   *Miniland USA*

This signature attraction of Legoland California is fun for the whole family.   Miniland is a collection of American landmarks from seven different geographical regions of the United States constructed with more than 20 million Lego bricks at 1:20 scale.

Miniland USA is located in the center of the park and has several entrances. It is a very large area. Be prepared for a lot of walking. The Lego scenes are depicted in amazing detail. Every time I go I see something that I hadn't noticed. During the holiday season all the Miniland areas are decorated with mini holiday decorations.

Seeing everything takes some time. Even the smallest members of your party may want to pause to discuss and contemplate their favorite scene. Destiny and Jared's favorite areas of Miniland include: the animated **New England (#19)** countryside with mini farm animals that come to life when your child pushes a button, and the **Dayton 500 International Speedway (# 90)** where guests help the Lego brick cars speed around the track. Throughout the rest of Miniland USA, there are buttons to push which trigger fun animated details. Bring some extra quarters so you can sail Lego boats in the **Miniland Marina (#86)**.

Adults will be fascinated by models of some of America's great cities.

- **Las Vegas (#80)** For kitschy fun check out Las Vegas which features the world famous Las Vegas Strip, complete with many of the Strip's luxury hotels, a wedding chapel, monorails, and a recording of the real sounds of Las Vegas. At certain times of day an Elvis impersonator "Las Vegas Concierge" puts on a cheesy lounge act with corny jokes and trivia questions about Legoland. The prize...an autographed picture of the Lego Concierge!

- **Washington DC (#81)** Looking at the model of Washington D.C. is a good way to introduce kids to our Nation's Capitol's important landmarks. These include the White House, Capitol Building,

Smithsonian, Washington and Jefferson Monuments and parts of Georgetown. Cherry trees bloom every spring along the Capitol Mall.

• **New Orleans (#84)** is alive with Mardi Gras, complete with parade floats and a fun calliope that the kids can play.

• The **New York (#85)** skyline is an important part of Miniland. The Freedom Tower already exists in the Lego universe. Commuters hurry about Grand Central Station. At Christmas time skaters circle the rink at Rockefeller Center.

• California is well represented in Legoland. **San Francisco (#87)** Victorian "Painted Ladies" are down the street from the Golden Gate Bridge. **Southern California (#88)** has some surfers catch some waves in San Diego. Hollywood makes an appearance as well.

• **Ferndale** is a little town in Northern California. Its Victorian structures have been preserved so its main street looks very much like it did in the 1800's. Rumor has it that Legoland was attracted to this town because it had many early settlers from Denmark. The picturesque Victorian buildings must have also made it an appealing representation of small town America. Legoland did not inform the town fathers of Ferndale that they were planning to build a model of their town. The editor of the local paper heard about its construction from the friend of an out of town subscriber.

Block of Fame (#82) – You know you are famous when you are represented in this Lego Block of Fame. Have your kids identify the famous individuals represented. It's a great history lesson.

Art of Lego (#89) – The Mona Lisa is made of Lego bricks? Salvador Dali and Andy Warhol are just some of the famous artists whose work is recreated in Lego bricks.

Model Shop (#83) – See the Lego magic in action by peaking into the Lego builder's workshop. This is definitely worth a look, but it's hidden towards the back of Miniland so seek it out. This is a fun activity for grownups.

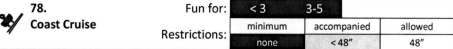

78. **Coast Cruise**	Fun for:	< 3	3-5	
	Restrictions:	minimum	accompanied	allowed
		none	< 48"	48"

This boat ride is cheesy fun for all ages. You can take in the sights of Legoland, see really interesting models, and have a fun time together as a family. The Coast Cruise is a great way to begin or end your trip to Legoland. The boat holds quite a few people at one time, so even a longer line won't take forever.

IX. Age Appropriate Activities

A. *Under 3 Years-Old*

Baby Care Center - (#29)

(Fun Town) Here is your home base when visiting Legoland with a baby or toddler. You will find a microwave, high chair, bottle warmers, rockers for nursing moms and baby change facilities.

The following is a list of attractions and rides appropriate for this age group. The items stared were Destiny and Jared's favorites during their toddler years.

- Dig Those Dinos (#8)
- Safari Trek (#10)
- ✪ Fairy Tale Brook (#11)
- Playtown Theater (#13)
- ✪ Water Works Magical Fountain (#15)
- ✪ Water Works Stomp and Spritz (#15)
- Village Theater (#16)
- ✪ Duplo Playtown (#17)
- ✪ Legoland Express (#18)
- Sky Patrol (#21)
- ✪ Fun Town Stage (#26)
- Fun Town Fire Academy (#31)
- Adventurers' Club (#34)
- ✪ Flight Squadron (#36)
- Skipper School (#37)
- ✪ Swabbies Deck (#40)
- Enchanted Walk (#46)
- Cargo Ace (#63)
- ✪ Duplo Play (#76)
- ✪ Coast Cruise (#78)
- ✪ Miniland USA (#79-91)

Cut here and take with you to Legoland ✂

B.   *Ages 3-5*

Legoland is ideal for this age group. There is so much to see and do!
Every time you return, your kids will get bolder and begin to try out the
more exciting rides. One challenge with this age group is that some
rides require a one adult per child ratio. Big kid chaperones don't count.
If a ride below is labeled "with parent", assume that you will not be able
to ride with two small children at the same time.

The following is a list current of favorites for Destiny (age 4) and Jared
(age 3).

- Coastersaurus (#7) (with parent)
- Dig Those Dinos (#8)
- Safari Trek (#10) (with parent)
- Fairy Tale Brook (#11)
- Playtown Theater (#13)
- Water Works Magical Fountain (#15)
- Water Works Stomp and Spritz (#15)
- Village Theater (#16)
- ✪ Duplo Playtown (#17)
- ✪ Legoland Express (#18)
- Kid Power Towers (#19)
- Sky Cruiser (#20) (with parent)
- Sky Patrol (#21) (with parent)
- ✪ Volvo Junior Driving School (#24)
- Fun Town Stage (#26)
- ✪ Fun Town Fire Academy (#31) (Maximum 4 people per truck)
- Lego Factory Tour (#32)
- Adventurers' Club (#34)
- Flight Squadron (#36) (with parent)
- Skipper School (#37) (with parent)
- Treasure Falls (#38)
- Soak-N-Sail (#39)
- ✪ Swabbies Deck (#40)

✂ Cut here and take with you to Legoland ✂

- Captain Cranky's Challenge (#41)
- Buccaneer's Booty (#42)
- Splash Battle (#43)
- Wild Woods Golf (#45)
- Enchanted Walk (#46)
- Builders' Guild (#47)
- The Hideaways (#50)
- King's Treasury (#51)
- Courtyard Theater (#53)
- ✪ The Royal Joust (#55)
- The Dragon (#58)(with parent)
- ✪ Beetle Bounce (#61)
- ✪ Cargo Ace (#63)
- Lost Kingdom Adventure (#64) (with parent)
- Pharaoh's Revenge (#66)
- Lego Technic Test Track (#69)(with parent)
- ✪ Aquazone Wave Racers (#67) (with parent)
- Lego Show Place (#71)
- ✪ Bionicle Blaster (#68)
- Bionicle Evolution (#72)
- Duplo Play (#76)
- Build & Test (#77)
- Coast Cruise (#78)
- Miniland USA (#79-91)

C.   *Ages 6-12*

Legoland can still be fun for this age group. There are a few thrill rides and lots of other fun activities. Number one on Justin's list is shopping for Legos! Here are other fun rides and attractions recommended by Justin age 9 and his friend Adam.

 Be sure to sign up for a Mindstorms session as soon as you hit the park.

- Coastersaurus (#7)
- Raptor Splash (#9)
- Safari Trek (#10)
- Village Theater (#16)
- Kid Power Towers (#19)
- Sky Cruiser (#20)
- ✪ Volvo Driving School (#25)
- Fun Town Stage (#26)
- Fun Town Fire Academy (#31)
- Lego Factory Tour (#32)
- Skyscraper Climb (#33)
- Adventurers' Club (#34)
- Skipper School (#37)
- Treasure Falls (#38)
- ✪ Soak-N-Sail (#39)
- Captain Cranky's Challenge (#41)
- Buccaneer's Booty (#42)
- ✪ Splash Battle (#43)
- Wild Woods Golf (#45)
- Builders' Guild (#47)
- ✪ The Hideaways (#50)
- King's Treasury (#51)
- Courtyard Theater (#53)
- ✪ The Dragon (#58)
- ✪ Knights' Tournament (#60)

✂ Cut here and take with you to Legoland ✂

- Beetle Bounce (#61)
- Lost Kingdom Adventure (#64)
- ✪ Pharaoh's Revenge (#66)
- ✪ Lego Technic Test Track (#69)
- Aquazone Wave Racers (#67)
- Lego Show Place (#71)
- Bionicle Blaster (#68)
- Bionicle Evolution (#72)
- Maniac Challenge (#73)
- ✪ Lego Mindstorms (#74)
- ✪ Build & Test (#77)
- Miniland USA (#79-91)

D.   *Fun Activities for the Whole Family*

With a 9 year-old and two preschoolers, we are always looking for activities that make everyone happy. Here is a list of some of our favorites. *(Minimum height 34")*

- ✪ Coastersaurus (#7)
- – Dig Those Dinos (#8)
- – Safari Trek (#10)
- – Fairy Tale Brook (#11)
- ✪ Playtown Theater (#13)
- – Water Works Magical Fountain (#15)
- – Water Works Stomp and Spritz (#15)
- – Village Theater (#16)
- – Sky Cruiser (#20)
- – Fun Town Stage (#26)
- ✪ Fun Town Fire Academy (#31)
- – Lego Factory Tour (#32)
- – Adventurers' Club (#34)
- ✪ Skipper School (#37)
- – Soak-N-Sail (#39)
- – Swabbies Deck (#40)
- – Captain Cranky's Challenge (#41)
- – Buccaneer's Booty (#42)
- ✪ Splash Battle (#43)
- – Wild Woods Golf (#45)
- – Builders' Guild (#47)
- ✪ The Hideaways (#50)
- – King's Treasury (#51)
- – Courtyard Theater (#53)
- – Beetle Bounce (#61)
- – Lost Kingdom Adventure (#64)
- ✪ Pharaoh's Revenge (#66)
- – Lego Show Place (#71)

Cut here and take with you to Legoland

- Bionicle Evolution (#72)
- ✪ Build & Test (#77) *The little ones can check out Duplo Sets*
- ✪ Coast Cruise (#78)
- ✪ Miniland USA (#79-91)

E.   *Rainy Day Activities*

Some fun indoor activities for a rainy day at Legoland are:

☐ **Lego Mindstorms (#74)** Be sure to sign up for a session as soon as you hit the park. For your older Lego fan age 9 and up, this will be a fun way to stay dry. Your child will program a robotic vehicle to perform specific tasks. I have enjoyed watching my son and his friends perform this task. It gives you insight into just how brilliant your kid really is!

☐ **Maniac Challenge (#73)** Kids will love playing fun Lego computer games. Our family favorite is Lego Island. It is a fun, non violent adventure by a young Lego mini-fig named Pepper. They also have Bionicle games, Lego Chess, etc. You can also check out Lego sets at the entrance. They range from easy to complex and some even have a motor! This activity will keep the whole family busy for quite a while. It is fun for your kid to give mom or dad pointers as you build with Lego bricks.

☐ **Bionicle Evolution (#72)** If you have a Bionicle fan, this may be the place for you. Thousands of pieces are available to construct a custom Bionicle.

☐ **Build and Test (#77)** Keep your child busy for a long time building and racing Lego brick vehicles. Younger siblings can join in the fun or can play with Duplo blocks and construct a Dora Lego set. Your family can also check out some award winning Lego creations on display from the Lego Junior Model Master Builder Competition.

☐ **Duplo Play (#76)** This is a great area to keep young children busy on a wet day. There are several areas with different types of Duplo blocks to build with. Even big brother or sister may have fun building towers and bridges.

☐ **Lego Show Place (#71)** Spell Breaker and Lego Racers 4D are exciting 4-D movies that provide some indoor distraction.

☐ **Pharaoh's Revenge (#66)** Take shelter in the fun play area, but be aware it's loud in here! Mom and dad may not want to stay very long.

☐ **Lost Kingdom Adventure (#64)** Part of the line for this ride is under cover, so if you can wait without getting wet, this would be a great bet for the family.

☐ **Builder's Guild (#47)** If you find yourself in Knight's Kingdom on a rainy day, you can take refuge in the Builder's Guild. This is an out of the way pavilion filled with an impressive Lego Castle and lots of tiny Lego bricks for construction.

☐ **Adventurer's Club (#34)** This is a short, but fun activity. Take a few minutes to walk through this world of Legos and look for the secret keys.

☐ **Lego Factory Tour (#32)** Take your time, watch the Lego factory video, then head off on the tour to see for yourself how Lego bricks are made. There are plenty of buttons for your little ones to press.

☐ **Lego Club House (#30)** In the corner of this store there is a free play area with lots of little Lego bricks for building Lego creations.

☐ **Playtown Theater (#13)** Legoland's new show, Journey to the Lost Temple, will provide 25 minutes of interactive musical fun. Be sure to check it out.

X.   Food: Where to Eat

Legoland's official policy is no outside food. As I have said previously, this policy is not consistently enforced so it is worth bringing snacks or a picnic for the family. In the event of a problem, it can be eaten on the grassy area outside the front gate.

If you are ready for a special treat, Legoland has lots of yummy restaurants. Membership Plus and Ambassador Members get 20% off all food at restaurants (not at snack carts). Make sure to flash your card. Since I am a budget conscious local, I have not sampled the food at every Legoland restaurant. The restaurants I have visited have been full of healthy choices and good quality food.   The portions tend to be generous as well. With my own experience and a little help from friends and online reviewers, here is a run down of Legoland restaurants. I have divided them into three sections to help you plan your culinary adventure: Yummy and Quick Snacks, A Quick Meal and Sit Down and Take a Break.

A.   *Yummy and Quick Snacks*

The Market (#6)

(The Beginning) This quick serve deli conveniently located at the entry courtyard of Legoland offers gourmet coffee, cappuccino, café latte, and espresso. It also has beverages, salads, and sandwiches to go. Craving something sweet? They also serve fruit flavor or chocolate swirl Dryer's soft serve ice cream. There is a limited amount of seating outside for you to stop and have your snack.

Although this location tends to be on the pricy side, for the caffeine dependent grownups in your party, there may be one bargain. Purchase a travel cup full of coffee for $9.95 and get free refills all day.

Popcorn and Popsicle Stands

(Explore Village by Storybook Boats; Dippin' Dots by Pirate Shores and Enchanted Walk on Castle Hill) For cheap treats, popsicles and juice bars are available with prices starting at $2.50. Frozen lemonade is offered at a slightly higher price. Explore Village also has a popcorn stand.

Lego Clubhouse (#30)

(Fun Town) This area offers Dryer's soft-serve ice cream, cold beverages, popcorn, and snacks. During Lego Club Weekend there is a two for one popcorn promotion at this location.

Granny Apple Fries (#49)

(Castle Hill) Granny Apple Fries is our favorite snack spot at Legoland. This sweet treat costs $4.35 and is a bargain because it can be shared by family members. The fried Granny Apples are dusted with cinnamon and sugar. They are served with a vanilla cream dipping sauce. Everyone in our family loves this treat. Eat at a table next to the restaurant or munch on a few of your very own while watching the kids play at the nearby Hideaways play area.

Fool Scoops (#54)

(Castle Hill) These huge ice cream cones cost $3.25. Fool Scoops also offers sundaes, frozen drinks, cappuccino, café latte, and espresso.

Hot Dog Stand

(Land of Adventure) This stand offers some of the more unusual entrees at Legoland. In addition to the traditional hot dogs and cold drinks it offers exotic hot dogs for $4.25. The Mediterranean gourmet hot dog is topped with hummus, onions, tomatoes, chopped cucumbers with a tsatsiki sauce and pita chips. The Far East Hot Dog is topped with wasabi mayo, daikon radish, and green onions. It has a teriyaki glaze.

B.   A Quick Meal

Burger Stop (#22)

(Fun Town) Located next to the Driving School, this hamburger stand sells burgers, cheeseburgers, and trans fat free fries.

Fun Town Hot Dogs (#28)

(Fun Town) This hot dog stand next to Fun Town Market serves Hebrew National Hotdogs with all the fixings.

Castle Burgers (#59)

(Castle Hill) Located next to The Dragon rollercoaster, this stand sells burgers, cheeseburgers, and trans fat free fries.

Pizza Mania (#75)

(Imagination Zone) This restaurant serves pizza, snacks, cold beverages, and soft serve ice cream. During the summer it also serves a Pizza Meal for $25.99 that would serve the family.

C.   Sit Down and Take a Break

Ristorante Brickolini (#14)

(Explore Village) This Italian restaurant offers wood-fired pizza, delicious pasta topped with homemade sauces, fresh salads, and desserts. It is home to the Fruizza, dessert baked and layered with fresh fruit. Brickolini offers courtyard dining. At the back of the courtyard there are two tented areas with low picnic tables for the kids, and regular tables for the grownups. Sometimes used for parties, if the curtains are open your family is welcome to dine there.

During the summer this restaurant has a really great dinner special. We think it's the best deal in the park. It is so huge, even with a family of 5 we still bring home leftovers! For $34.95 you get a great pizza with choice of toppings including some really yummy looking veggies or just cheese if you are serving picky toddlers, big drinks that you can refill, and a choice of sauces (during our visit it was marinara and pesto) The pesto was delicious! I've also heard that their alfredo sauce is excellent. A big "anti-pasto" salad with choice of dressing was included. We enjoyed the salad, but in the future will ask them to hold the green olives and pepperochinis. The meal included a decent amount of breadsticks, and a brownie or tiramasu for dessert. Ken enjoyed this dinner so much, he keeps wanting us to go every time he doesn't like what's on the Smith family dinner menu ☺. It is definitely a "Dad's Pick".

Fun Town Market Restaurant (#27)

(*Fun Town*) Located at the back of Volvo Driving School, this is a great buffet restaurant where you can meet the needs of almost everyone in your family. Food is prepared fresh and features specialties such as oriental chicken stir fry, Philly cheese steak sandwiches, a well stocked soup and salad bar, baked goods, and Hägen-Dazs ice cream. Expect a wide variety of high quality, although not necessarily inexpensive, food.

Knights' Table Barbecue (#52)

(*Castle Hill*) Looking for a table in the shade and some down home comfort food? Located on Castle Hill, this restaurant offers a hearty fair of spare ribs, fire roasted chicken, baked beans, corn on the cob, salads, and more. If you are extra hungry you might want to consider attending the Pirate's Feast which is an all you can eat barbecue buffet. Try a little of everything for $18.95 for adults and $8.95 for kids. A pirates feast combo admission ticket is also available. See the website for details.

Upper Deck Sports Café (#70)

(*Imagination Zone*) Want a chance to enjoy "sit down" dining with the hope the kids will actually let you eat your dinner? Try the Upper Deck Sports Café located in the Imagination Zone. This full service restaurant has a Lego brick playroom. Upper deck is a Carlsbad sports memorabilia company and a lot of Upper Deck products are displayed as part of the décor. The menu tends towards the upscale including salmon burgers and carne asada nachos, but also offers kids favorites.. This is the restaurant most equipped to accommodate those with special diets or food allergies.

The Garden Restaurant (#92)

(Officially in Miniland but just next to Pirate Shores) This restaurant is located by Pirate Shores overlooking Miniland. It specializes in providing healthy options including gourmet sandwiches, homemade soups, and salads. I haven't eaten here, but the web reviews were very good.

D.   *Food Allergies/Dietary Concerns*

This is the one area where Legoland officially permits you to bring outside food for special medical needs. However, it may be possible to purchase what you need inside the park. Legoland posts specific information regarding meals that accommodate various dietary needs on its website http://www.legoland.com/park/Dining/dietaryconcernsmenu.htm. This includes information regarding gluten free and nut free foods and restaurants as well as vegan and vegetarian options available at the park. E-mail or call, using contact information on the above webpage, 72 hours ahead of time to ensure that Legoland can meet your needs.

XI. Shopping in Legoland

Legoland, like all theme parks, has plenty of opportunities to spend money. There are a wide variety of shops located throughout the park. Some of the attractions end in a shop which seems to be the new trend in theme park design. Thankfully, most don't and those that do are easy to exit quickly if you are not ready to spend your money.

What I appreciate about Legoland is that it offers fun souvenirs at all price ranges. Of course you can purchase a number of really great and unique Lego sets, but there are also lots of fun toys and dress up items that reflect the themes of each Legoland area.

If you are planning to purchase souvenirs, take a few minutes to read this section and get an overview of what's available. With a little preplanning you can find a lasting memento of your day at Legoland, rather than grabbing the first thing you see, that will be tossed in the toy box and forgotten when you arrive home.

Left the park, but realize that you really wanted to purchase one more souvenir? You can show your credit card and get a Legoland shopping pass. If you return to show your receipt before the hour is up, your credit card is not charged for admission. If you can prove that you spent more than $20, your parking will also be refunded.

If you are looking for a bargain, know that you can get 20% off of your purchase of $10 or more if you show your Membership Plus or Ambassador card. I have seen individual items discounted and displayed in the front window of the Big Shop.

A. *The Stores*

Purchases made at any of these stores can be transferred to the front of the park, and you can pick them up on your way out. Take advantage of this service, and you can enjoy the rides instead of dragging your purchases around the park.

The Big Shop (#4)

(The Beginning) This is the biggest store at Legoland, and it has tons of merchandise. It is always crowded, so keep your little ones close! This is a great place to stop on your way out of the park, but be aware that at closing time, it gets very busy. This shop has a great overall assortment of Lego Sets. It occasionally has specials displayed in the window. Last time I was at Legoland, The Big Shop was offering a $20.00 Bionicle set for $10. They also offer some small Lego sets and mini-fig key chains for less than $10. If you don't see the character set that you are looking for, you might want to check the Studio Store in Fun Town or the Pippin's Bazaar gift shop in Land of Adventure for the latest in Indiana Jones Lego sets.

Dig Those Dinos (#8)

(Dino Island) If your child loves dinosaurs make sure you check out this shop. It contains lots of fun dinosaur and paleontologist memorabilia. You can also rent a shovel and pail to go dig for dinosaur bones in the sand pit. Kids get a special surprise when they return their shovel

Studio Store (#12)

(Explorer Village) This store has lots of Lego licensed products, like Bob the Builder, Sponge Bob, Indiana Jones, Star Wars and Batman. For a fee, you can also record your own audio CD. There are a few items here that are under $20 including character mini-fig key chains and mini-fig magnets.

Lego Clubhouse (#30)

(Fun Town) This store at the end of the Lego Factory tour has lots of Lego bricks in bulk ($7.99 per ¼ pound) and make and create sets. It also has some fun items like Lego Lollypops and Lego key chains. You can also grab an ice cream or some popcorn at this location.

Brick Brothers Trading Company (#35)

(Fun Town) You're in California...so why not look the part? This shop stocks surf clothing and accessory brands like Quicksilver and Roxy.

Buccaneer's Booty (#42)

(Pirate Shores) This store sells bathing suits, hats, T-shirts, towels, and sunscreen. It also stocks pirate gear. It is a good place to get a temporary tattoo if that strikes your fancy.

King's Market (#57)

(Castle Hill) This is a fun eclectic shopping area. Pan for Crystals, have your name written in colorful picture letters, or pick up the latest gear for knights and princesses. Each booth has a surprise in store. The face painting booth is also very popular. Some of the booths can be pricy so watch out. A princess up doo with tiara and makeup was $40.00!

Pippin's Bazaar (#65)

(Land of Adventure) This Store located by the Lost Kingdom ride has lots of inexpensive fun explorer themed trinkets and a large assortment of Indiana Jones Lego sets.

B. *Other Places to Shop and Pay to Play*

Caricature Booths

These are located throughout the park. The artist draws an exaggerated portrait. The prices are as follows $20 just your head, $25 head and body, and $15 per person if you are doing a family portrait. Since this is obviously a substantial investment, visitors to the park have recommended that you observe several artists and choose the one you like the best before commissioning a portrait. The artist can hold the portrait for you until you leave the park so you don't have to worry about it being soaked or bent.

Games by Pirate Shores

Here you can do some traditional carnival games and win prizes. Little guys can fish out rubber duckies. Big kids can throw basketballs, baseballs, or play a skeet ball like game, in order to win prizes.

C. *Free Stuff*

- ☐ Drop in to Member Services and pick up the latest issue of Lego Magazine.
- ☐ You can often pick up a small trinket at the end of the Lego Factory Tour.
- ☐ Get a commemorative Lego brick by participating in the monthly Jr. Master Builder competition.
- ☐ Attend Brick or Treat for commemorative bricks, candy, and other treats.
- ☐ Lego pass holders can pick up a monthly commemorative brick from the Lego Club House.
- ☐ Attend Lego Star Wars Day and receive a commemorative brick.

D. *Member Discounts*

Membership Plus members, Resort members, Ambassador members, and Resort Ambassador members receive a 10% discount on most store merchandise.

XII. Sea Life Aquarium

My family and I visited this aquarium during its first weeks of operation. Perhaps they are still working out some of the kinks! It was a fun activity, but I found myself wishing that it had more hands on activities or perhaps more fish to look at. There are areas that have very few tanks, and just a lot of murals and informational posters. It has two fun tide pool areas, but the sides are so high, that my two children who were a little over 3 feet tall, couldn't reach in and touch anything. They each required a substantial boost to get down to the water. A well placed stool or step would have really been appreciated. The facility is designed like a labyrinth and it was very difficult to keep track of my 3 year-old as he raced from room to room. There was a fun quiz trail activity that kept my son engaged, but the questions were very difficult to spot. I have included some clues that should help you find them in the exhibit descriptions that follow.

My kids are rather spoiled, they grew up in Santa Cruz which is less than a mile away from the world renowned Monterey Bay Aquarium. This aquarium has an amazing collection of aquatic creatures, but it also has a wonderful hands-on preschool area that is both educational and fun. I guess I expected something similar as I visited the Sea Life aquarium so I came away a little disappointed.

Should you include a visit to the Sea Life Aquarium in your visit to Legoland? I would say that it depends on what else you will be doing on your trip to San Diego. If you are planning to visit Sea World, you might want to skip the Sea Life Aquarium. Sea World's exhibits are very impressive, well thought out, and much larger. If you have transportation you could also head down the coast and visit the Birch Aquarium in La Jolla at UC San Diego. The admission is half of the price and the parking is free. The exhibits are more detailed, and there are interactive exhibits that might be more fun for both your older school-aged and teen-aged kids. Family days are held at the Birch aquarium the third Saturday of each month from 11 am - 3 pm. These offer lots of fun interactive family activities that teach kids about the ocean using art and literacy themes.

All that being said, if you are not planning to visit either of these venues or have preschool or young school aged children, this aquarium is a great way to introduce them to the wonders of the ocean. What makes this aquarium different (other than the cool Lego creatures and scuba divers distributed throughout) are the fun ways that kids can get "up close" with the fish swimming in the tanks. Many areas either have bubble windows that look into the tank or up under the tanks. Other tanks have peep holes towards the bottom of the tank so kids can see things on their own level. Still others provide steps to climb on so that little kids can enjoy the same view as the grown ups. For those of us who are used to constantly lifting our children so that they can enjoy similar venues, this kid friendly design is very much appreciated.

If you are planning to visit both Legoland and the Sea Life Aquarium you will want to purchase the Park Hopper pass which will save you almost $9 on Sea Life admission. Plan on seeing the aquarium in about two hours. Try and go at a less popular time of day. We started our visit around 4 pm and didn't find it to be too crowded. I don't think that the aquarium would be very enjoyable during more crowded times. If you see a big line outside the aquarium it might be worth coming back at another time.

The Sea Life Aquarium exhibits include several that reflect California aquatic fresh water and marine ecosystems. It also has a whimsical Atlantis area filled with colorful tropical fish.

Before you enter the aquarium, enter the door to the café, go upstairs, and take a bathroom break. This is the only bathroom. It cannot be accessed inside the aquarium. You can also use the outdoor restrooms located to the right of the aquarium. Accessing any bathroom once you enter the Sea Life Aquarium is difficult if near impossible.

A.   *The Exhibit*

The Entrance

You start your journey into the Sea Life aquarium, in small dark crowded room with many other people. I kept losing my active preschooler in the crowd. An introduction comes over the loudspeaker that asks you to imagine that you are a member of a research expedition that will be exploring the ocean. The voice outlines the rules: no flash photography, no food or drink, and no banging on the windows. It mentions the quiz trail. Make sure you have a quiz card and map before proceeding to the first exhibit.

Lake Tahoe

The highlight of this exhibit is a small bridge and children's slide constructed over one of the tanks of cold water fish indigenous to Lake Tahoe. Fish displayed include trout, catfish, and bass.

San Francisco Harbor

The fish in this area are indigenous to the San Francisco Bay. One of the neatest parts of the exhibit is a 3 foot octopus hiding out in one of the tanks. My kids also enjoyed crawling into a boat which contained portholes that gave them another perspective of the tank. They could also stand up in a bubble in the middle of a tank, and make funny faces at the fish.

 You will find question #1 which pertains to global warming on the wall as you enter this exhibit.

California Coast

The California coast exhibit has a small kelp forest and represents an ecosystem similar to that found in the Monterey Bay. You can watch bright orange garibaldi, rock fish, eels, and kelp fish swim. There is also a tide pool (this one is not a touch pool).

 Question #2 has a picture of an octopus.

Kelp Forest

This area contains no tanks, but contains interesting information about kelp. The walls of the exhibit are covered by gigantic pictures of the kelp forest taken by a local photographer. Fun activities in this area include checking your own height and comparing it to the speedy kelp growth. On the wall as you leave are magnetic fish that you can move around the kelp forest.

Shoaling Ring

In this area you are surrounded by a circle of sparking Silver Mono, a fish indigenous to Africa, Asia, and Australia.

Theater

This is a small theater with comfy seats. BBC videos about the ocean are shown continuously.

Southern California Tide Pool

This tide pool contains a fun variety of cold water critters. Kids have the opportunity to touch sea snails, sea cucumbers, and starfish. My smaller kids found it challenging to reach far enough to touch the critters. Be prepared to give your child a boost. You can also see if the docent could bring one close to the side.

 Question #3 is on the wall with a picture of a starfish. Question #4 is located on a surfboard.

Sea Life Lab

The focus of this exhibit is ocean exploration.

 Question #5 on gray whale migration is located at the entrance to this exhibit.

Lost City of Atlantis

This is one of the most elaborate exhibits at the Sea Life Aquarium. The tanks are filled with colorful Lego divers. There are videos about Lego explorers visiting Atlantis. My son Jared enjoyed pushing buttons to make lights go on and Lego divers move around.

My favorite area in the whole aquarium was a walk through tank. You could see the fish swimming overhead. My daughter Destiny appreciated the low port holes that gave her a better view of the action. It was fun to see a white-tip reef shark swimming among the ruins of Atlantis.

Ship Wreck

In this exhibit your Lego explorer gets to look inside a shipwreck. Brightly colored tropical fish including clown fish, tangs, and eels hide among the "artifacts". The coral in these tanks is beautiful and has brilliant colors! There is an observation area where you can sit back, take a rest, and enjoy the main tank.

 Question #6 is about artificial reefs. Question #7 at the top of the stairs has a picture of a shark

Surf Break

The Surf Break area contains several tanks of fish.

Ray Lagoon

This was a fun area. Kids have a chance to learn fun facts about rays and watch as the rays swim around their gigantic tank.

 Make sure you go behind the tank. Question #8 is located there. Kids can also peek through the low peepholes get a closer view of the swimming rays.

Kingdom of the Seahorse

Sea horse conservation is one of the areas of focus for the Sea Life organization. This exhibit has very interesting information about seahorses and a wide variety of sea horses.

 Question #9 is on the wall as you enter. The answer is on the wall as you exit the exhibit.

Discovery Zone Touch Pool

The Discovery Zone Touch Pool is a fun way to end your Sea Life adventure. There is a large touch pool with a many types of sea snails. In the adjoining pool hermit crabs scurry about. Destiny marveled at their brightly colored purple and orange feet. There are also some fun tanks. Kids can climb into the final tank and look through a bubble as the fish swim around their head.

 The final question regarding toxic waste is located across from the touch pool.

B.   *Ocean Journey Café*

You can start your day here with a $10 breakfast buffet. The restaurant also serves lunch and dinner. The Ocean Journey Café has good food with lots of salads and pastas. This restaurant has a nice layout that includes indoor and outdoor seating. There is a colorful Duplo brick play area for the kids.

C.   *Gift Shop*

This shop contains lots of Ocean related stuffed animals and toys. It also has a few Lego themed items.

XIII. What Else to do in Carlsbad California

A. *Beaches*

Carlsbad has a number of great beaches with lots of free parking. Just be willing to park on some sand or walk in. The two closest to Legoland are:

North Carlsbad State Beach (*Tamarack*)

This beach has a convenient parking lot right on the beach. It is currently free, but may soon charge a parking fee. A big sea wall provides a great place to walk, jog, or stroll along the water without getting too sandy. Life guards are on duty during the summer. Grab some takeout in nearby Carlsbad Village and have a beach side picnic.

South Carlsbad State Beach (*Ponto*)

This beach is usually less crowded than Tamarack. It is currently more isolated; however, a big hotel and shopping complex will soon be constructed across from the beach. Lifeguards are on duty during the summer. You can park on the sand in designated areas. You might need to get creative! There is also a pay parking lot. Be prepared for a hike to the bathrooms and wear shoes, since you have to cross some rocks to get there. Our family likes to hit this beach in the evening when it is less crowded.

B. *Museum of Making Music*

5790 Armada Drive
Carlsbad, CA
(760) 438-5996

This Museum sponsored by the NAMM foundation (the philanthropic arm of the International Music Products Association) explores the history of music products in America. Some visitors have enjoyed seeing some beautiful instruments and exploring the interactive exhibits. Others have found the museum to be less than kid friendly. I would say if you have a school-aged child who enjoys music and is mature enough for a museum visit this may be worth checking out. Kids enjoy the last room in the museum where they can play instruments with headphones on.

C. *Flower Fields*

5704 Paseo Del Norte
Carlsbad, CA
(760) 431-0352

This is a fun outing for families with younger children. Adults will enjoy the splendor of The Flower Fields as well. It may be a harder sell for older elementary aged kids, preteens, and teens. Located just minutes from Legoland, this is a working flower farm. Every spring a Carlsbad hillside blooms with over 50 acres of Giant Tecolote Ranunculus flowers. This is a breathtaking sight. The Flower Fields offer beautiful gardens, tractor rides through the fields, fun play equipment inspired by Santa's Village, and a collection of rare Poinsettias. There is even a garden of Lego flowers! If you are planning a visit, you may want to hit The Flower Fields before going to Legoland. Last time we were there we were able to get a coupon for free child admission with the purchase of an adult admission. The Flower Fields are open March-May. Visit their website www.theflowerfields.com.

D. *Parks*

Friday evenings during the summer, the City of Carlsbad sponsors concerts in various parks around Carlsbad. See the city of Carlsbad website for more info. www.carlsbadca.gov.

Aviara Park

6435 Ambrosia Lane
Carlsbad, CA

This park is always hopping with lots of kids and their parents. It has swings and a great climbing structure, picnic tables, and lots of grass for running or playing ball. The bathrooms are well maintained, and within easy access to the playground.

Poinsettia Park

6600 Hidden Valley Road
Carlsbad, CA

The play structure at this park is a little on the older side, but kids have fun climbing and sliding anyway. The bathrooms are right next to the playground which is a plus. The really fun part of this park is that it is filled with rolling grassy hills. My kids love to roll.

Holiday Park

Corner of Chestnut Ave. and Pio Pico Dr.
Carlsbad, CA

This park has fast slides, swings, and plenty of places to climb. It is shady, so it's a good park to visit on a hot day. Located off Highway 5 across the freeway from Carlsbad Village, Holiday Park is a fun place to have a picnic and get kids energy out.

Pine Avenue Park

Harding Street, bordered by Pine and Chestnut
Carlsbad, CA

This park has nice play structures for kids age 2-12. A heated bathroom is nearby. It has lots of grass to run on. This park is located within walking distance of Carlsbad Village.

Skate Park

2560 Orion Way
Carlsbad, CA
(760) 434-2851

This skate park is great for beginning and intermediate skaters. Safety gear is required, so bring your helmet, knee pads, and elbow pads. The skate park is located between the fire station and the police station just off of El Camino Real about 10 minutes from Legoland.

Have a more extreme skater and are willing to pay to skate? The Magdalena Ecke YMCA Skate Park in Encinitas is an amazing place to skate. Click on programs on the YMCA website for more info: www.ecke.ymca.org. Helmets, elbow, pads and knee pads are required so bring them along!

E. *Shopping*

Carlsbad Premium Outlets

5260 Paseo Del Norte #100
Carlsbad, CA
(760) 804-9000

If you enjoy bargain hunting, the swanky Carlsbad Premium Outlets may be for you. It has 90 outlet stores for upscale brands including, Vans, Ann Taylor, Sketchers, Etnie, Gap and Gap Kids, Lucky Brand Jeans, and Juicy Couture. Local moms swear by the bargains at the Osh Kosh B'Gosh, Baby Gap and Gymboree outlets. Your tween surfer or skater can pick up the latest styles and gear at the Sun Diego Board shop. They also have a Learning Express Toy Store for the little ones. This is also home to the kid friendly Ruby's Diner.

Carlsbad Village

Carlsbad Village Drive and State St.
(Multiple blocks)

Carlsbad, CA
(760) 434-2553

Carlsbad Village has free parking and lots of fun boutiques and bookshops. You can also check out the weekly Farmer's Market for delicious food and crafts.

The Forum

1923 Calle Barcelona
Carlsbad, CA
(760) 479-0166

This upscale outdoor shopping center is a fun place to stroll and window shop. Kid friendly stores include a big Border's Books, Geppetto's Toy Shop, and a Cold Stone Ice Creamery.

F.   *Snug Harbor / Fox's Lagoon*

California Watersports

4215 Harrison Street
Carlsbad, CA
(760) 434-3089

Like water sports? At Snug Harbor/ Fox's lagoon you can canoe, water ski, or ride a wave runner. Prices range from $15 an hour for kayak rentals to $125 an hour for waterskiing.

G.   *Batiquitos Lagoon*

Nature Center

7380 Gabbiano Lane,
Carlsbad, CA
(760) 931-0800

Ready for a nature walk? Batiquitos Lagoon provides a kid friendly walk and a chance to learn more about the local ecosystem. Start at the nature center close to the Gabbiano Lane entrance. If it's not open, you can still pick up an interesting trail guide. On our first visit, my 7 year-old loved reading the guide and telling me about all the plants and animals that lived in the Lagoon. The trail takes you on a journey past the freeway with trucks rumbling by (my preschoolers love this part). You move past posh vacation homes, and then end up in the wilderness. This path is popular with dog walkers and joggers. There are no bathrooms, so plan accordingly. In a kid emergency, a country club about half way along the trail has been known to let weary families use their public bathrooms.

H.   *Carlsbad Library*

Dove Branch

1775 Dove Lane
Carlsbad, CA
(760) 602-2038

Carlsbad's Dove library is a beautiful complex that includes an auditorium and free art gallery. It offers fantastic summer programs for kids, including science activities, movie nights, and magic shows. Check out the library website www.carlsbadca.gov/library and click on the programs and events calendar for more information.

I.   *Golf*

The Crossings at Carlsbad

5800 The Crossings Drive
Carlsbad, CA
(760) 444.1800

www.thecrossingsatcarlsbad.com

Golf isn't the most kid friendly activity, but grownups should be able to have fun on vacation too. This new public golf course is just up Palomar Airport Road directly adjacent Legoland. It has been named by Golf Magazine as one of the top ten courses you can play.

The Four Seasons Aviara Resort Golf Course and the La Costa Resort and Spa also offer world class golf courses and are located close by.

J. Play Werx

6060 Avenida Encinas #B
Carlsbad, CA
(760) 804-1600

Only in Carlsbad...an indoor kids play area with a café that offers fair trade organic coffee, espresso, organic raspberry lemonade, and healthy organic snacks. Admission is $10 for kids 4 and up , $5 for kids 3-and-under, and adults are free. Think upscale Chuck E. Cheese. Pricey, but if you find yourself in Carlsbad with hyper kids on a rainy day, it might be worth a visit.

K. U-Pick Strawberries

Corner of Cannon Rd and Paseo del Norte
Carlsbad, CA

Just off of Cannon Road, east of Interstate 5 you can pick your own strawberries. The U-Pick season runs mid spring to July. Check out the Carlsbad Strawberry website for more information www.carlsbadstrawberrycompany.com.

L. Leo Carrillo Historic Park

6200 Flying LC Lane
Carlsbad, CA
(760) 476-1042

Leo Carrillo was a film and television star from the 1950's. He once owned a large ranch in Carlsbad. You can tour the historic buildings on site. There are also lots of hiking trails. On summer Friday nights Leo Carrillo films are shown in the barn.

XIV. Family Dining in Carlsbad

Al's Café "In the Village"   795 Carlsbad Village Dr
Carlsbad, CA
(760) 729-5448

Al's is a great neighborhood diner. Kids are welcome. It also offers free samples of fudge. What more could a visitor to Carlsbad want?

Benihana   755 Raintree Dr.
Carlsbad, CA
(760) 929-8311

This would be a great restaurant for an adventurous older kid. Benihana is a Japanese grill where a chef cooks most of the food right at your table. It's not just a dinner it's an entertainment experience! They have a kids meal for kids 10-and-under for $7.95. It contains smaller portions of Benihana's regular fare. Don't expect to find hamburger or macaroni and cheese here!

Buca di Beppo   1921 Calle Barcelona
Carlsbad, CA
(760) 479-2533

Ready for a sit down dinner with a twist? Buca di Beppo is a chain restaurant with décor so interesting it just may keep the kids occupied until dinner arrives. Family sized portions make dining fun. My friend recommends asking for the kitchen table so the kids can watch their food being prepared.

Cessy's Taco Shop 3016 Carlsbad Blvd
Carlsbad, CA
(760) 434-2648

This taqueria was recommended by a fellow Carlsbad mom. Rumor has it local surfers enjoy the breakfast burrito. The shrimp quesadilla also has a great reputation

Claim Jumper 5958 Avenida Encinas
Carlsbad, CA
(760) 431-0889

The prices are on the high side for a chain restaurant, but almost every entrée can feed more than one person. You may not need to spring for the kids meal. My friend, the mom of three, recommends coming for happy hour and feeding everyone appetizers.

Islands Restaurant 889 Palomar Airport Rd
Carlsbad, CA
(760) 602-9898

This tropical themed restaurant is great for kids and very close to Legoland. Surf, ski, and skateboard videos keep the kids occupied while waiting for their food. Crayons and coloring sheets are provided. The rowdy atmosphere means that families are welcome. The food is good and the menu contains some healthy kid's options.

Karl Strauss Brewing Company 5801 Armada Dr.
Carlsbad, CA
(760) 431-2739

Yes, it's a brew pub. That also means that it is nice and noisy so your brood won't be noticed. Reviewers think the food is good and the proximity to Legoland is a plus.

Pat and Oscar's

965 Palomar Airport Road
Carlsbad, CA
(760)-929-7040

Pat and Oscar's offers delicious pizza, fresh salads, and the best breadsticks ever. This restaurant has lots of room to spread out, fast service, and a gumball machine by the door. Pat and Oscar's is just down the street from Legoland (next to Costco) and is a great way to finish up the day.

Pollos Maria

3055 Harding St.
Carlsbad, CA
(760) 729-4858

If you are looking for neighborhood taqueria. Pollos Maria is the place for you! It serves yummy roasted chicken and other Mexican specialties. The tamales were a little dry, but everything else I've tasted has been yummy. Lots of my friends are big fans of this local dive. It is very casual so feel free to bring the kids.

Ruby's Diner

5630 Paseo del Norte
Carlsbad, CA
(760) 931-7829

This fun fifties themed diner has good food and great service. There is a train encircling the dining room that keeps the kids mesmerized. Rumor has it that they have even had someone making balloon animals upon occasion. Ruby's has a great location in the Carlsbad Premium Outlets close to Legoland and The Flower Fields.

TGI Fridays

890 Palomar Airport Road
Carlsbad, CA
(760) 431-5009

TGI Friday's has a prime location across the street from The Carlsbad Flower Fields and just off Highway 5. Look for the giant windmill. You can't miss it! This location has a reputation for being kid friendly.

That Pizza Place

2622-6 El Camino Real
Carlsbad, CA
(760) 434-3171

This restaurant is a ways from Legoland, but is super kid friendly so it is worth a mention. It is a small town pizza joint. The walls are covered with funny ads and memorabilia. It has arcade games in the back, as well a race car and a horsie to ride. Good pizza and a salad bar top off this fun locale. It is a favorite with neighborhood soccer and baseball teams, so it may be busy when you visit.

Tip Top Meats

6118 Paseo del Norte
Carlsbad, CA
(760) 438-2620

Breakfast or dinner in a butcher shop? Sure it's unconventional, but for lots of food at a great price you might just want to give it a try. This butcher shop with adjoining restaurant serves breakfast, lunch, and dinner cafeteria style. Dining is available inside and out, so you are sure to find a spot that works for the kids. The food is German inspired. Be prepared to try sauerkraut and beets, homemade sausages and big slabs of meat. There is also a selection of tempting pastries for dessert and it's located close to Legoland.

Village Kitchen and Pie Shop

950 Tamarack Ave.
Carlsbad, CA
(760) 729-6414

This restaurant is a local favorite. Located just east of Highway 5 off of Tamarack Ave, the Village Kitchen and Pie Shop serves up affordable home cooking. The portions are generous and the pie comes highly recommended.

Index:

CPSIA information can be obtained at www.ICGtesting.com
Printed in the USA
BVOW071806230113

311381BV00002B/597/P